CONTENTS

ACKNOWLEDGEMENTS

The original version of this Guide was written by Derek O'Carroll, advocate and was published by the Chartered Institute of Housing in Scotland, July 2000. In preparing the original version he gratefully acknowledges the assistance provided by Andrea Moore and Alan Ferguson of the Chartered Institute of Housing in Scotland, the substantial support and encouragement of Alan R. Dewar, advocate and Julia Maguire, solicitor, the helpful comments made on the original draft by Paul Brown, solicitor, as well as those made by others in the consultation process. He is also grateful to Simon Collins, advocate, for permission to draw from several of his ideas contained in a conference paper. The original version of this Guide was funded by the Scottish Executive.

This version of the Guide is based on the original version by Derek O'Carroll and has been updated and adapted for England and Wales by Sam Lister. In preparing this version Sam Lister would like to thank Lorna Findlay, barrister, at St Philips Chambers, Birmingham and Helen Tucker, solicitor, at Anthony Collins Solicitors, Birmingham for their helpful comments on the draft.

Any errors are those of the authors, however. The Guide has been updated to 30 July 2001.

ABOUT THIS GUIDE

The original version of this Guide was published by the Chartered Institute of Housing in Scotland in July 2000 with support from the Scottish Executive. This latest version is based on the original text but is intended for use in England and Wales. It has been updated to take account of developments in the courts since the Act came into force on 2 October 2000, which have clarified a number of issues which the original could only raise as points of speculation. The Guide has also been expanded to take account of aspects of housing law which at the time of writing have no Scottish equivalent, for example introductory tenancies.

The Guide is intended to be a readable, concise introduction to the main provisions of the legislation and the consequent housing management issues that may arise. It is intended for use by housing professionals, particularly those working in the public sector and for registered social landlords. This Guide is designed to give the reader a general understanding of the Act, together with examples of how it is likely to be applied to some common housing management problems. Its aim is to equip the reader with a broad enough understanding to be able to apply the principles of the Act to new problems and issues as they arise. The general overview it provides is intended to complement the forthcoming publication *Human Rights for Housing Officers: A Guide to Proofing Day-to-day Practice* (CIH/JRF, 2002), which will act as a training resource book for housing organisations as well as a procedural guide to auditing and proofing local policies and procedures.

This Guide is not, and cannot be, a comprehensive statement of the law. In particular, only those aspects of the legislation which are likely to impact directly on the housing professional in the delivery of housing services are addressed. Neither can this Guide, given the constraints of space, provide very much in the way of detailed analysis of the issues contained within. Further information can be obtained from the references in the footnotes and the sources noted at Section 6 of this Guide.

HOW TO USE THIS GUIDE

This Guide is designed in the following way.

The **Introduction** (Section 1) contains a detailed summary of what the Human Rights Act 1998 says and its likely effects. Those who are **newcomers** to the subject will find this a helpful introduction. It also contains recommendations on how to do a human rights audit. Those who want to know only the basics of the Act need read no further.

Section 2 provides more **detailed discussion of some key areas** of the Act. Those interested in a fuller examination of those areas may find it of help. Those who do not need this can ignore it.

Section 3 examines each of the **four Convention rights** which will be of most relevance to housing issues. This Section will be of help in understanding the fourth Section.

Section 4 examines a number of areas of **housing law and practice** and comments on the extent to which, if at all, the Act is likely to have an effect. This Section will be of the most direct interest to housing professionals. Many readers may want to begin their reading at this point and then go back to some of the earlier Sections.

Section 5, Enforcement of the Act, looks very briefly at how the Act is enforced.

In Section 6, there is a list of **further sources and references** and websites.

Following the main part of this Guide in **Appendix 1** is the **abridged text of the Convention rights** which are incorporated in the Act.

An **Index of Cases** referenced in the footnotes can be found in **Appendix 2**. The table in **Appendix 3** provides a summary of the **key housing cases** that have been decided under the Human Rights Act 1998 since it came into force on 2 October 2000.

The purpose of the **footnotes** is only to provide references, sources of authority and further explanation and clarification of points in the text *should the reader need them.*

1: INTRODUCTION TO THE ACT

1.1   **Background.** The Human Rights Act 1998[1] (referred to throughout this Guide as "the Act") was passed in 1998 and is intended to be a keystone of the Government's policy of constitutional reform. The Act came into force on 2 October 2000. One reason for the delay was to give those affected by the Act, such as the courts, the Government and other public authorities, time to adjust their activities and procedures. The length of delay itself indicates that much was needed to be done to ensure compliance. It should be noted that the Act will also apply to some decisions and actions of local authorities made before 2 October 2000 which are the subject of legal proceedings taking place after that date. The National Assembly for Wales and its functions (including its ministers) have been subject to the terms of the European Convention on Human Rights ("the Convention") since May 1999.[2]

1.2   **Whom the Act applies to.** The Act applies to all "public authorities" in the UK.[3] This term is defined very widely.[4] It includes all courts and tribunals. It also includes all Government departments, local authorities, quangos and non-departmental public bodies. It includes at least some activities of registered social landlords.[5] Virtually every decision taken by a local authority is potentially affected by the Act. In particular, the main functions of local authorities, such as education, social work, planning and environmental regulation, licensing and housing, are all directly affected in some way by the Act.[6] The purpose of the Act is to provide certain safeguards for the individual citizen and private organisations (such as companies) as against the state and organs of the state. What it does *not* do, in general terms, is create direct rights for private individuals as against each other.[7] In other words, a complaint by an individual that

---

[1]   The full text of the Act can be found in any one of the sources listed in Section 6 of this Guide.
[2]   Government of Wales Act 1998, Section 107.
[3]   See Section 6 of the 1998 Act.
[4]   Section 6(3).
[5]   See below at paragraph 2.1.2 for further discussion of whom the Act applies to.
[6]   See in particular Articles 5, 6, 8, 9, 10, 11, 14 of the Convention on Human Rights, and Articles 1 and 2 of the First Protocol (an amendment) to the Convention.
[7]   In general terms, this is true. However, in certain cases, the Act imposes a positive duty on public authorities to take action so as to ensure that one private individual does not lose rights as a result of another individual's actions: see Section 2.3 of this Guide. In addition, since the courts and tribunals are under a duty also to apply the Act, there will be an indirect effect especially as far as the common law is concerned.

his/her Convention rights have been broken can usually be made only if s/he can identify an action or omission by a public authority which caused that breach.

1.3   **Effect of the Act.** The purpose of the Act is *not* to incorporate the Convention into British law. What the Act does is enable individuals and private organisations to invoke Convention rights in the UK courts for certain purposes and for limited effects. It also makes unlawful all actions by a public authority which are "incompatible with a Convention right".[8]

1.4   **Background to the Convention.** The European Convention on Human Rights[9] is an international treaty, under the aegis of the Council of Europe, signed by the United Kingdom (one of the first signatories) in November 1950. The European Union (and its Court of Justice and other institutions) is quite separate from the Council of Europe (and its European Court of Human Rights). The Convention (whose original content was heavily influenced by lessons drawn from the Second World War) sets out certain fundamental rights and freedoms which all the signatory states guarantee to their citizens and private organisations. Each statement of a right or freedom is contained in a separate Article.[10] All the signatory states are European or within the European sphere of influence. The signatory states between them have a wide range of social, economic and cultural backgrounds. The Convention rights thus, to a certain extent, represent the lowest common denominator. In many areas, the rights already enjoyed by citizens of the UK are superior to the minimum guarantees in the Convention. The rights and freedoms guaranteed are principally civic and political rights rather than social and economic rights. There is, for example, no guaranteed right to work or to housing contained within the Convention.[11] Over the years, the Convention has been amended by 11 "Protocols".

1.5   **Former procedure for claiming a Convention right.** Formerly, a person who wished to complain that s/he had not been treated by a public authority in accordance with the Convention first of all had to attempt to get satisfaction in the UK courts, applying *Scottish or English law*, not the

---

8   Section 6(1). With the exception of those actions which a body is compelled to carry out by statute.
9   More formally known as the Convention for the Protection of Human Rights and Fundamental Freedoms.
10   In this Guide each reference to a numbered Article is a reference to that Article of the Convention or to a Protocol to the Convention: see the end of this Guide for the text of the Convention rights including the First and Second Protocol.
11   And so in many respects, English law goes further than the Convention – for example, the homeless persons legislation contained in Part VII of the Housing Act 1996.

Convention rights (since the Convention had never been part of either Scottish or English law).[12] If that failed, the person had a right to lodge a complaint that the Convention had been breached by the UK Government with the European Commission of Human Rights. The Commission would then consider whether the complaint was admissible.[13] If so, the Commission would issue an advisory opinion on the merits of the case, which was not binding on the Government. The case then went to the European Court of Human Rights (referred to throughout this Guide as "the ECHR") for a final decision. The process could take years, and frequently did.[14] The Commission and the ECHR have now been merged, creating, in effect, one single court.[15] This process was obviously unwieldy and likely to produce injustice. Furthermore, it resulted in a relatively large number of successful complaints to the ECHR, which did little for the international image of the UK.[16]

1.6   **The Convention rights.** From 2 October 2000, when the Act came into force, the position is rather different. At the core of the Act are most of the Articles of the Convention containing statements of the fundamental rights and freedoms guaranteed by the Convention.[17] In summary,[18] these are as follows:

---

[12]   While this is strictly true, since *R v Home Secretary, ex parte Brind* [1991] 1 AC 696 at 747 there have been many instances of the English courts taking the Convention into account when making a decision on a case. See, for example, *Attorney General v BBC* [1993] AC 534 and *R v Khan* [1996] 1 WLR 162. The Scottish courts were somewhat more reluctant to do the same (*Kaur v Lord Advocate* 1981 SLT 322, (Scottish courts to take no account of the Convention)) but the judicial climate changed somewhat in 1997: (*T Petitioner* 1997 SLT 724: (if legislation ambiguous, assume that Parliament intended to legislate in conformity with the Convention)).

[13]   The admissibility threshold is high: only about 1 in 10 complaints were ruled admissible: see Reid (1998), pages 10 and 19. This suggests that there may be a similarly high failure rate in the courts when the Act is in force from 2 October 2000.

[14]   Delays of four or five years were not uncommon. This is ironic in view of Article 6 of the Convention, which guarantees the right to judgments within a reasonable time.

[15]   Consisting of 4 types of composition. See the Eleventh Protocol, which came into force on 1 November 1998. See Reid (1998), pages 7 and 8 for the new procedure.

[16]   Most other signatory states allow some form of access to their own courts for challenge of decisions on Convention grounds. Measures that the UK Government was forced to introduce into UK law as a result of successful challenge include: the Interception of Communications Act 1985; the Security Service Act 1989; the Children Act 1989; the end of the criminalisation of homosexual acts between consenting adults over 21; the end of corporal punishment in public schools, among many others.

[17]   The most significant omission is Article 13, which guarantees the right to an "effective remedy" before the national courts for a breach of the Convention. The Government's stated reason for omitting this provision is that the enacting of the Act itself ensures compliance with the Convention. Not all commentators agree. One effect of the omission is that the national courts are limited in the orders they can make in the event that they find that there has been a breach of the Convention. See further Section 5 of this Guide and note 236 below.

[18]   See the end of this Guide for the full text.

The fundamental rights and freedoms guaranteed by the Convention.

Article 2	Right to life
Article 3	Prohibition on inhuman and degrading treatment
Article 4	No slavery or forced labour
Article 5	No unjustified detention
Article 6	Right to fair hearing: civil and criminal matters
Article 7	No retrospective penalties for criminal offences
Article 8	Right to respect for home life, privacy, the home and correspondence
Article 9	Freedom of thought, conscience and religion
Article 10	Right to freedom of expression
Article 11	Right to freedom of assembly and association
Article 12	Right to marry
Article 14	No discrimination in relation to Convention rights
First Protocol: Article 1	Right to peaceful enjoyment of possessions
First Protocol: Article 2	Right to education[19]
First Protocol: Article 3	Right to free elections
Fourth Protocol	No capital punishment

The Articles that will be most relevant to housing providers are Articles 6, 8, 14 and Article 1 of the First Protocol.[20]

1.7 **How the Convention rights will be applied in England & Wales.** The Act specifies the way in which these Convention rights are to be applied in the UK. The most important are summarised as follows.[21]

Key features of how the Human Rights Act 1998 applies the Convention:
- **Interpretation.** All legislation must be interpreted and applied, so far as it is possible to do so, in a way which is compatible with the Convention rights.[22]
- **Public authority duty.** All "public authorities" (see Section 2.2 below for meaning of public authority) must act in a way compatible with Convention rights unless primary legislation (such as an Act of

---

[19] This right is qualified by a "Reservation" obtained by the UK Government: see Schedule 3, Part II to the Act.
[20] See Section 3 of this Guide for a detailed examination of these Articles.
[21] See Sections 2 and 3 of this Guide below for more detail.
[22] Section 3.

Parliament) makes this impossible.[23] All actions of local authorities are covered, whereas only some activities of RSLs may be covered.[24]

- **Victim**. Only a person or organisation who can show that s/he/it is a "victim" of a breach of a Convention right may rely on the Convention in legal proceedings.[25]
- **Remedies**. A person or private organisation claiming that s/he/it is a victim of a breach, by a public authority, of a Convention right may complain to the courts or raise that issue in the context of other legal proceedings.[26]
- **Power of the courts**. If the court or tribunal finds that there has been a breach of a Convention right, the court may make any order, within its powers, as it considers "just and appropriate".[27] This may involve the award of compensation if necessary to give "just satisfaction". The court cannot, however, overrule primary legislation: it may only make a declaration of "incompatibility".[28] It will then be up to the Government to put amending legislation to the UK Parliament if it considers that there are "compelling reasons" for doing so.[29]
- **ECHR caselaw**. The courts and tribunals, when considering any question involving a Convention right, must "take into account" the caselaw of the ECHR.[30]
- **Certain rights emphasised**. Particular importance is placed on the right to freedom of expression and freedom of thought, conscience and religion.[31]
- **Limitation**. A victim of an alleged breach of a Convention right must commence proceedings within one year of the alleged breach.[32] However, there is no restriction as to time where the Act is raised as a defence to proceedings brought by a public authority (e.g. possession).[33]

---

[23] Section 6.

[24] See further comment at Section 2.2 of this Guide below.

[25] Section 7(7), which imposes the same test as would be applied by the ECHR under Article 34 of the Convention. See below at Section 2.4 of this Guide for further detail.

[26] Section 7. Thus, the person claiming to be a victim may seek judicial review of an action or omission of a public authority, injunction and interim injunction, or seek to raise that issue in the context of another court case: for example, as a defence to an eviction action (claiming, perhaps, that his/her rights to respect for his/her home (Article 8) have been breached).

[27] Section 8.

[28] Section 4.

[29] Section 10, Schedule 2.

[30] Section 2. That is, the caselaw is not binding on the court. It is highly likely, however, that the ECHR caselaw will, where relevant, be highly influential, at the very least, on the UK courts. It follows that when a public body is considering the lawfulness of any action that it has taken, or proposes to take, it too must take account of the ECHR caselaw.

[31] i.e. Articles 9 and 10. See Sections 12 and 13.

[32] Or a shorter period if otherwise usual. For example, Employment Tribunal proceedings must usually be commenced within three months of the act complained of. The court has the power to extend the one-year period if "equitable in all the circumstances" (Section 7(5)). There is no time limit with regard to raising devolution issues under the Government of Wales Act 1998.

[33] See Section 7(1)(b) & 7(5).

- **Timescales**. Although the Act did not come into force until 2 October 2000, certain actions or omissions of a public authority may be invoked as a Convention defence whenever they took place.[34]
- **Duty on courts etc**. The courts and tribunals are public bodies and must therefore apply the Act in all their actions.[35] Special provision is made for challenge of court and tribunal actings.[36]
- **ECHR application right preserved**. The right of an individual to take a case to the ECHR in Strasbourg is preserved: but, as at present, the UK court process must first be exhausted.[37]

1.8 Consequences for public housing providers.

1.8.1 The effect of the Act on public authorities, including housing providers such as local authorities, Government departments (for example, the Defence Housing Executive) and, possibly, registered social landlords,[38] is likely to be great. They have a clear duty under the Act to comply with the Convention rights. At least four of the Convention rights are directly relevant to housing providers (see Section 3.1 below). The duty is to interpret legislation, where possible, so as to comply with Convention rights. Only if that cannot be done, because primary legislation prohibits it, can it act in a way incompatible with the Convention. It may still end up being challenged in the courts, however, if the aggrieved person wishes to seek a declaration of incompatibility.[39]

1.8.2 Where the housing provider has discretion, as is very common in housing legislation, that discretion must be exercised with a clear eye to the relevance, if any, of the Convention. Housing providers, who are subject to the Act, must make decisions proactively in accordance with the Act. This includes not only a decision in relation to a particular application or request by a tenant (for example, for an exchange of tenancy), but any other actions which are capable of affecting a person's Convention rights, for example:

---

[34] Sections 7(1) and 22(4). If, however, a person claiming to be a victim of a breach of the Convention raises legal proceedings, the action or omission must have taken place on or after 2 October 2000. See further below at Section 5 of this Guide.

[35] This provision may have a profound influence on the common law. Since the courts are bound by the Convention, they may not make a decision contrary to it unless forced to do so by statute. There is no such restriction in respect of the common law. See further Lester and Pannick: *Human Rights Law and Practice*, para. 2.6.3.

[36] Section 9.

[37] Section 11: which also preserves all existing rights of action that any person or private body may have at the moment.

[38] See below at Section 2.2 of this Guide for discussion as to which bodies are likely to be public authorities for the purposes of the Act and, in particular, whether registered social landlords are included.

[39] See Section 5 of this Guide for more details.

- Policy formation (such as allocation policies and eviction policies: but the list of such policies is potentially huge).
- Instructions to housing officers.
- Council resolutions.

It is not sufficient to examine a decision for compatibility with the Convention only if it is challenged.

1.8.3 The net effect of this is that all public housing providers are strongly advised to carry out a human rights audit of their entire housing management systems, policies and procedures. At the very least, such an exercise would involve the following process:

- Provision of detailed training on the Act to senior management initially.
- A comprehensive examination of all housing policies, practices, procedures and documentation (including tenancy agreements) to check for compliance.
- Identification of risk areas and assessment of degree.
- Taking of expert legal advice especially in areas of uncertainty or high risk.
- A planned, timetabled and monitored rectification programme of change in those areas found to be deficient.
- Training for all those involved in the provision of housing, from board level downwards, on the Act and the changes to policy, practice and procedure.

1.8.4 Public housing providers should have been applying the Act even before 2 October 2000, as any policies and decisions made then which are still "live" will be actionable now if the Convention is breached. Furthermore, the Convention can be invoked as a defence in respect of any legal action in progress after 2 October 2000, regardless of when the act complained of took place.[40] Following implementation of the human rights audit, adherence to the Act must be continually monitored, not least because of the living nature of the Convention.[41] This monitoring should include at least the following:

- Scrutinising all proposed changes to policies and practices to check for compliance with the Act.
- Setting up internal mechanisms so that the experience of all staff, and concerns about Convention compatibility of the organisation's policies, are fed back to senior management for decision.

---

[40] See note 33 above.
[41] See paragraph 2.6.8 of this Guide.

- Monitoring of developments in Scottish, English and ECHR caselaw, taking specialist legal advice where appropriate.

For further guidance on conducting a human rights audit see *Human Rights for Housing Officers: A Guide to Proofing Day-to-day Practice* (CIH/JRF, forthcoming 2002).

1.9 Likely future developments.

1.9.1 Public housing providers should, however, recognise that the nature of the Convention is the provision of minimum guarantees in certain areas of civil and political life. It represents the lowest common denominator of the rights which the individual can expect as against the public bodies. In many areas, the UK qualifies as one of the more advanced countries in the Council of Europe. Many, if not most, of the laws and procedures followed by public authorities in England and Wales conform to, and exceed, that minimum standard. The introduction of the Act will probably not lead to wholesale reform of the substance of English law. What is more likely is that the Act will have a significant effect on procedure, processes and institutional culture, particularly because of the application of the "Convention tools".[42] It can be expected that there will be many legal challenges advanced against public housing providers, and other public authorities, which will, at the very least, test the law. Some will be successful.

1.9.2 It is difficult to say at this early stage exactly how the courts will approach human rights cases. Although the ECHR has decided thousands of cases, these decisions are not binding on the courts (although they are likely to be persuasive at the least).[43] Furthermore, as explained below, the principles of interpretation of the Convention rights by the ECHR include the granting of a degree of discretion (the "margin of appreciation") to the state, and that degree of discretion varies according to the issue involved. Other principles of interpretation of the Convention which may also be adopted by courts (see Section 2 below) will make it harder to predict how the courts will react to challenges brought before them. In addition, the caselaw of the courts in other countries with similar laws may be used by the parties or the courts as an aid to interpretation. Of the limited cases heard so far one pattern that is beginning to emerge is that the courts are reluctant to grant declarations of incompatibility against Government legislation which is the clear will

---

[42]   That is, the tools of interpretation used by the ECHR in interpreting the Convention: see further Section 2.6 of this Guide.

[43]   Section 2, the obligation is to take "into account" the caselaw of the ECHR.

of Parliament. Conflict between the Government and Parliament on one side, and the judiciary on the other is being avoided by making full use of the margin of appreciation where the Convention permits it.[44] It may be that during the early years the courts will adopt a more cautious approach, partly in response to criticism from the popular press that the Act will work only to promote "liberal" issues and will mostly "benefit criminals who will use human rights defences as a matter of course".[45]

1.9.3 The consequence of all this for the public housing provider is that the Act presents new and uncertain territory in which the boundaries are unclear. It is accordingly not possible for anyone at this stage to state definitively how the law will develop over the next 10 years. But develop it will. The precautions recommended in Section 1.8 above may not guarantee the absence of a successful challenge on human rights grounds. However, a failure to apply what is known of Convention law and to demonstrate at least an attempt to comply will almost certainly result in successful challenges against public housing providers. In the context of housing matters, there are a number of possible areas of challenge which are more fully explored below at Section 4. First, however, this Guide explores more fully some of the aspects of the Act referred to in this Introduction.

---

[44] In particular recent legislation designed to deal with anti-social behaviour such as Introductory Tenancies under the Housing Act 1996 or the use of Anti-Social Behaviour Orders under the Crime and Disorder Act 1998, *R (on the application of Johns & McLellan) v Bracknell Forest District Council*, [2001] 33 HLR 45; *R (on the application of McCann) v Manchester Crown Court* [2001] EWCA Civ 281. See Sections 4.5 and 4.9 of this Guide.

[45] See, for example, *Daily Telegraph*, 4 August 2000, for a critique of the Act and how it will interfere with the democratic will of Parliament.

2: Some Key Points Expanded

This Section explains in more detail some key concepts which are relevant to understanding how the Act will work. It is not necessary to read this Section if all that is required is a general understanding of the Act.

2.1 What is a public authority?

2.1.1 This is a key question since it is primarily public authorities that are subject to the Act. The Act does not define what a "public authority" is; it merely imposes obligations on it and then states that the term includes both courts and tribunals[46] and "any person certain of whose functions are functions of a public nature". The Lord Chancellor has stated that this Section has been deliberately left wide so that the fullest application of the Act can be made.[47] The Government White Paper on the Human Rights Bill says the same.[48] Local authorities, the National Assembly for Wales and the UK Government departments[49] are certainly public authorities, as are Housing Action Trusts and regulatory bodies such as the Housing Corporation. [50]

The extent to which independent social businesses, the voluntary sector and other quasi-public sector bodies are affected is less clear. Difficult questions as to the extent of the Act are likely to arise with "hybrid bodies" which have both public and private functions. The fact that a body performs services on behalf of a public body will not in itself be

---

[46] Tribunals which are of special relevance to housing professionals include Social Security Appeal Tribunals (for housing benefit appeals), Rent Assessment Committees, Leasehold Valuation Tribunals and the Lands Tribunal.

[47] *Hansard* H L, 19 January 1998, Col. 1262. See further Lester and Pannick, para. 2.6.3 for detailed analysis.

[48] CM 3782 'Rights Brought Home: The Human Rights Bill' (July 1997) at para. 2.2. "The definition of public authority is wide. It includes central Government (including executive agencies), local government, police, immigration officers, prisons, courts and tribunals and, to the extent that they are exercising public functions, companies responsible for areas of activity previously in the public sector such as privatised utilities."

[49] Including executive agencies such as the Rent Service or, in Wales, the Rent Officer Service, who are part of the functions of the National Assembly.

[50] Other regulatory bodies of relevance to housing professionals include the National Assembly for Wales (regulating Welsh RSLs), The Housing Inspectorate, the Benefit Fraud Inspectorate, the Local Government Ombudsman and the Independent Housing Ombudsman.

conclusive evidence that they are performing a public function.[51] However, where a hybrid body is performing a public function they will only be a public authority to the extent that they carry out that function.[52] For example, Railtrack will be a public body when it acts in its role as the regulator and not when it acts in a private capacity, such as in its relationship with its employees or when entering into other contracts.

2.1.2 **Registered social landlords and housing associations.** The position of RSLs is complicated and despite an early decision from the courts the matter is still far from clear cut. The question is whether they are bodies "certain of whose functions are functions of a public nature".[53] The approach adopted by the courts appears to be that in determining whether a particular act is a public function will depend upon the extent to which it is "enmeshed in the activities of a public body".[54] This will be a matter of fact and degree and so will vary according to the exact circumstances.

It seems that despite the fact that RSLs are: subject to strict regulation by the Housing Corporation/National Assembly; the recipients of public funding; likely to have their core activities motivated by the public interest (e.g. charitable objects), and; may be formed entirely by the transfer of stock from a parent local authority (LSVT); are not themselves sufficient reasons to make RSL primary activities public functions. Regulation on its own does not mean that the activity being regulated is a public function. For example, banks are subject to regulation by the Bank of England, but they are still clearly private bodies. Neither does the fact that an RSL has been created by a transfer of local authority stock through LSVT automatically imply that its core activities are public functions, even where there is a continuing close working relationship with the parent local authority. The position seems to be that RSLs will only be public bodies in relation to a limited number of specific activities which have a particular "public stamp or character".[55] For example, an RSL who assists a local authority in carrying out its Housing Act duties to the homeless by providing interim accommodation pending its enquiries, including recovering possession on behalf of the authority following an adverse decision. In this particular example, the public nature of the activity would be even clearer if the transfer of the local authority stock which

---

51 See *Donoghue v Poplar Housing and Regeneration Company & The Secretary of State for the Environment, Transport and the Regions* [2001] EWCA Civ 595. For example, a private contractor carrying out services on behalf of a local authority.
52 Section 6(5) and *Donoghue*.
53 Section 6(2)(b).
54 See *Donoghue*, above.
55 See *Donoghue* above.

formed the RSL took place whilst the duty to the homeless applicant was ongoing.[56] However, the fact that this single activity is deemed to be a public function does not mean that all the activities of the RSL are also public functions.

2.1.3 Even where an RSL or other landlord is not performing a public function the Act still may have an impact on their activities. For example, the courts have a duty to act in a manner which is compatible with the Convention and where they fail to do so their decision could be judicially reviewed and quashed by the High Court. For example, if the court unreasonably refused to allow an adjournment in possession proceedings to allow the defendant to prepare their defence. [57]

2.2 Which actions of public authorities are subject to the Act?

This question can be broken down into two parts. First, what kinds of actions are affected? Second, what areas of activity are covered?

2.2.1 Section 6(1) of the Act simply says that it is "unlawful for a public authority to act in a way which is incompatible with a Convention right". Section 6(6) says: "an act includes a failure to act". Accordingly, both acts and omissions are covered. A failure to act in a way compatible with a Convention right is as unlawful as a positive action which is incompatible with a Convention right. Furthermore, there is no clearly defined limit on what acts are covered. Accordingly, not only decisions made by housing officers in relation to a particular tenant or applicant are included, but also a wide range of other matters are potentially covered. These could include matters such as the formulation of housing policies, instructions given to housing officers, the contents of documents such as tenancy

---

[56] The whole of this example is taken from *Donoghue* and seems consistent with a long line caselaw in this area. See *Peabody Housing Association v Greene* (1978) 38 P&CR. 644 (housing association in landlord/tenant dispute not judicially reviewable) and *R v West Dorset Housing Association, ex parte Gerrard* (1994) 27 HLR 150 (the Association was a competent party to a case involving homelessness rights). See *R v Panel on Take-overs and Mergers, ex parte Datafin* [1987] QB 815, CA, which held that in deciding whether a particular body was susceptible to judicial review, it was necessary to ascertain among other things what the functions of that body are, and where its powers come from. However, no one factor was decisive and the weight to be attached to each factor will vary in different cases. See *O'Reilly v Mackman* [1983] 2 AC 237, HL (appellant against prison visitors' decision not permitted to raise action based on public law in an ordinary action); *Cocks v Thanet District Council* [1983] 2 AC 286, HL (homelessness decision by local authority was public law; the implementation of the decision was private law). But see *O'Rourke v Camden LBC* [1998] AC 188, HL (following *Cocks* in its finding that a homelessness decision was public but overruling *Cocks* in so far as the private law classification of the implementation was concerned; i.e. there is no private right of action even once the homelessness decision is made).

[57] *Bates v London Borough of Croydon* [2001] EWCA Civ 134.

agreements and contracts made by the housing organisation. The wide range is subject to two limits. First, for the Act to be applicable, the act of the housing organisation must of course be one that breaches a Convention right of an identifiable person.[58] There must be a person who can claim to be a "victim".[59] Second, as the next paragraph shows, between RSLs on the one hand, and local authorities on the other, there is probably a difference between the areas of activity in which acts are affected.

2.2.2   The areas of activity covered by the Act probably differ according to the type of housing organisation. In Section 2.1 above, it was concluded that RSLs will very possibly be seen as a kind of hybrid body: part public and part private for the purposes of Section 6 of the Act. Therefore, in terms of Section 6(5), actions taken by an RSL which are concerned with the "private functions" of the RSL would fall outside the scope of the Act. Such actions may include building and renovation of housing for sale, provision of factoring services to the private sector, dealings with suppliers and employment contracts. Where the RSL has built houses using entirely private finance and then manages them, that will probably not be a public function. If so, the Act would not apply to such an RSL so far as that activity is concerned.[60]

2.2.3   The position as regards local authorities, and their housing departments, is different. Local authorities are, of course, creatures of statute.[61] The functions of the local authorities are entirely governed by statute. Their function is to perform a range of regulatory duties, provide services to the public in their area, collect rates and council tax etc. Their housing functions are governed by a number of statutes.[62] The housing provided by them is for the public, particularly those who have only modest incomes. The allocation of its housing is constrained by statute.[63] Accordingly, all the housing functions of a local authority will be public and therefore subject to the Act.

2.2.4   It is thought by some commentators that a local authority is a "pure" public authority, so that it does not fall into the Section 6(5) exception.

---

[58]   Which includes a private organisation such as a company or association.

[59]   See below at Section 2.4 for more detail on who is a victim for the purposes of the Act.

[60]   Whether a housing association is a charity does not alter the basic position but the aims of the charity will be relevant in deciding whether the function of the RSL is public or private.

[61]   Local Government Act 1972, Local Government (Wales) Act 1994.

[62]   Mainly, the Housing Act 1985, the Local Government and Housing Act 1989 and the Housing Act 1996.

[63]   Notably by the allocation and homelessness provisions in Part VI & VII of the Housing Act 1996.

Therefore, it is said, the Act applies to all functions of the local authority, not only those having a public element.[64] For example, disputes involving individual contracts of employment are what the courts would traditionally regard as private matters, even where the employer is a public sector employer. The usual rule, applied by both the English and the Scottish courts, is that where the subject matter is a dispute about the individual contract of employment, no judicial review is possible since the subject of the dispute is a private matter and not one in which the courts (exercising their supervisory function) will intervene.[65] By contrast, while the ECHR also characterises a particular employment contract as a private matter, it has been willing to apply the Convention to the rights of individual *public sector* workers as against their employer.[66] If that is so, it might well be that, so far as local authorities are concerned (and, by extension, presumably central Government and the courts), all areas of activity are covered by the Act, even those which the courts in the UK have traditionally regarded as "private" matters.[67] Other commentators take a different view.[68]

2.2.5 **Conclusion.** It remains to be seen what view the courts will take of this issue. It is likely that all actions of local authorities, Government departments, the Housing Corporation and the National Assembly will be affected by the Act. For RSLs, the critical issue is the nature of the function which the action complained of was intended to promote.

---

[64] See, for example, Supperstone et al. (1999), page 34 and the comments in Lester and Pannick para. 2.6.3. Contrast with the more cautious view by Carter, *Employment and Labour Relations Law*, in Baker (1998) at page 394.

[65] See *West v Secretary of State for Scotland* 1992 SC 385.

[66] Because the fact that the employer was the State enabled a complaint to be made to the ECHR. In an Article 6 claim, that meant that the dispute was a "civil" dispute and therefore justiciable by the ECHR: see, for example, *Darnell v UK* (1991) 69 DR 306 (NHS employee) and *C v UK* (1987) 54 DR 162. For further analysis of this, see Prof. Gillian Morris, *The Human Rights Act and the public/private divide in employment law* [1998] 27 *Industrial Law Journal* 293. See also Baker (ed.) (1998), Chapter 13. See *Alison Halford v UK* (1997) 24 EHRR 523 (policewoman: sexual harassment case where the police then bugged her private phone calls: Article 8 of the Convention).

[67] The difficulty with this is that this invents a new category of public authority which is not expressly mentioned in the Act: the "pure" public authority. Furthermore, this new category has duties over and above any other public authority since it (unlike a public authority where only some of its functions are public) is subject to the Act in all aspects of its functioning, whereas the part-public authority is only subject to the Act as regards its public functions. In effect, this interpretation brings private law matters into the jurisdiction of the Act simply because of the identity of the actor. One consequence is that an RSL and a local authority might make the same decision (say, in relation to a building contract), awarding it on obviously discriminatory grounds (say, the membership of a particular sectarian organisation). The local authority would always be potentially liable to a successful Convention claim; the RSL only if it was exercising a public function in awarding the contract.

[68] See, for example, Manning and Kilpatrick on *Acts of Public Authorities* in Baker (1998) at page 106.

The RSL will have to look at the whole circumstances surrounding the action. For example, what is being done, why it is being done, whether the action is being done in pursuance of a statutory power or obligation, whether there is a business element and whether issues of public policy are concerned. For RSLs, it is likely that only those actions connected with the exercise of a public function are affected by the Act.

2.3 Does the Act apply to acts or omissions by individuals?

2.3.1 The answer will usually be no. The object of the Convention, and therefore the Act, is to guarantee rights and freedoms of individuals (and private bodies and groups of individuals) as against the state and state organisations. The Convention does not guarantee rights for such individuals as against other individuals. So if, for example, the *Sun* invades the privacy of a princess by publishing risqué photos of her and her lover, her only remedy is under English law and not a complaint under Article 8 of the Convention. However, the ECHR has decided in some cases that the Convention must sometimes be interpreted so as to impose "positive" obligations on the state. That is, in some circumstances, the ECHR has found that a state has been at fault, not because it carried out the action, but because it failed to put into place measures to prohibit or prevent the act.[69],[70]

2.3.2 The Articles where positive obligations on the state have been found include Article 8 (right to respect for home and private life etc.). It is possible that a failure by a housing authority or an RSL to take action to stop anti-social behaviour would form a valid complaint under the Act.[71] However, in such cases, the state has always been given a wide "margin of appreciation" (i.e. discretion: see below at paragraph 2.6.1)[72] and the courts may also be reluctant to imply positive obligations on public authorities where there already lies an effective private remedy such as a private complaint of nuisance.[73]

---

[69] For example, in *Costello-Roberts v UK* (1993) 19 EHRR 192 the court decided that the UK Government was responsible for corporal punishment in private schools because it had a positive obligation with regard to the provision of education under Article 2 of the First Protocol to the Convention. The cases indicate that where an important individual right is at stake and the applicant is suffering significant effects a positive obligation may arise. However, where the individual interest is not perceived by the court as suffering material prejudice, or where an important interest of the state is at stake, it is less likely that the state (or public authority) would have a positive obligation. The courts may also be reluctant to imply a positive obligation where the aggrieved party has a clear private remedy such as in nuisance. See, for example, *Mowan* Section 4.8 of this Guide at notes 211 & 214.

[70] See Reid (1998), page 38.

[71] See Section 4.8 of this Guide below for further discussion.

[72] See, for example, *Rees v UK* 9 EHRR 56.

[73] See *Mowan*, note 214 below and Section 4.8 of this Guide below.

2.3.3   There is also the related question as to whether the Act will have a "horizontal effect": that is, whether if no public authority at all is involved, the courts should apply the principles of the Act to dealings between private individuals. Views on this question are divided and the question is in any event outside the scope of this Guide.[74] This will be one of the most interesting questions to be raised in the courts. Depending on what view is taken, the effect of the Act may be radically different from what is presently envisaged. Housing professionals and their advisers will particularly wish to keep abreast of developments in this area.

2.4   **Who is entitled to make a complaint under the Act?**

Only a person (or group of individuals or private organisation) who is a "victim" of an alleged violation of a Convention right and who would be entitled to make a complaint to the ECHR is entitled to raise the matter of an alleged breach of a Convention right in the UK courts.[75] The ECHR has defined "victim" fairly narrowly.

> The person claiming the violation must be affected personally and concretely. Thus representative organisations, such as pressure groups or tenants' associations, would not be able to raise legal proceedings unless it itself was the victim of some alleged violation.[76] There would be nothing to stop the individual members of that tenants' organisation from taking such action if they can individually show they have a personal interest in the alleged violation.

Arguments which focus on the alleged general injustice or unfairness of a measure or policy will not succeed alone. It is not necessary for actual prejudice or detriment to have occurred.[77] In a number of cases, it has been held that a *risk* of being directly affected is enough.[78] So, for

---

[74]   See further the following. Lord Irvine, in the House of Lords, thinks that it will have: *Hansard* 24 Nov 1997, Col 783 as does Sir William Wade (a constitutional law expert). See *The UK Bill of Rights*, a conference paper given at the Cambridge Faculty of Law 17/18 January 1998. Contrast with views of Michael Beloff in Betten (1999), *The Human Rights Act 1998: What it Means*, Martinus Nijhoff Publishers. See also G. Phillipson, 1999 MLR 824. See also Hunt, *The Horizontal Effect of the Human Rights Act* [1998] Public Law 423.

[75]   Section 7(7).

[76]   Companies, trades unions, churches, professional associations and political parties have all established "victim" status in various cases where they could show that their interests as organisations, as distinct from their members' interests, were at stake (see Baker (1998), page 41).

[77]   The ECHR has taken the view that whether actual prejudice or detriment has occurred is relevant to the question of remedy; i.e. if there has been no prejudice, it is unlikely that compensation will be awarded even in the event of a successful claim; see for example *Eckle v FRG* (1982) 5 EHRR 1.

[78]   For example, in *Campbell and Cosans v UK* 4 EHRR 293, the mere attendance of pupils at a school where corporal punishment was used was held to be sufficient risk of degrading punishment.

---

example, if a local authority housing provider were to pass a policy banning exchange of tenancies following a relationship breakdown, all its tenants who were in a relationship might be entitled to claim a violation of Article 8, not just those whose relationship had broken down and who wanted to apply for an exchange. Arguably also, all other tenants might be able to claim victim status. If the damage were remedied before the claim was decided (for example, the policy was changed), then the persons would lose their victim status.[79]

2.5 How English legislation and common law should be interpreted under the Act.

2.5.1 Section 3 of the Act says that "so far as it is possible to do so, primary legislation and subordinate legislation must be read and given effect in a way which is compatible with the Convention rights". "Primary legislation" includes Acts of the UK Parliament. Subordinate legislation includes regulations (such as those made by a Secretary of State or the National Assembly), rules and bye-laws made under primary legislation.[80] It applies to all legislation whenever it was passed.

2.5.2 The Act does not allow primary legislation to be overruled or ignored or have its validity affected. Nor does it allow secondary legislation to be ignored if the primary legislation under which it was passed prevents this.[81] It will, however, permit secondary legislation to be ignored where it cannot be read in a way which is compatible with the Convention.

2.5.3 The Lord Chancellor has explained this as follows:

> We want the courts to strive to find an interpretation of legislation which is consistent with Convention rights so far as the language of the legislation allows and only in the last resort to conclude that the legislation is simply incompatible with [it].[82]

2.5.4 Where it is not legislation, but the common law that is in issue, no such restrictions apply. The courts will be bound to interpret the common law consistently with the Convention where a Convention question arises. This will result in consequential changes to the common law. It also, of course, means that all public authorities will have to apply the Act rather than the common law.

---

79 See *Eckle* note 77 above.
80 Section 21.
81 Section 3(2).
82 *Hansard*, House of Lords, 18 November, 1997, Col 535.

2.6   What is the effect of the ECHR caselaw?

Section 2 of the Act says that the courts and tribunals should take into account the caselaw of the ECHR. Below are set out some of the principles that the ECHR applies when interpreting the Convention. The principles are a way for the Court to decide how any of the Convention rights should be given effect: if at all.[83]

2.6.1   **Margin of appreciation.** The Court allows each state a certain amount of discretion, the "margin of appreciation", to decide the best way of dealing with particular issues of interpretation in many of the Convention Articles. Providing that the state operates within that margin of appreciation, the ECHR will not interfere. The rationale is that Europe is a disparate collection of differing traditions and that, within limits, the state is in a better position to decide. This is similar, but not identical, to the concept of discretion that the courts afford to public bodies in judicial review cases.[84]

2.6.2   **Autonomous concepts.** The ECHR is not bound by the way that a state legal system classifies a particular concept. For example, the ECHR, when considering what is meant by a civil right or obligation, has decided that this means a "private right or obligation".[85] In deciding whether a particular obligation is private or public, the Court will consider the essence of the right that is at issue rather than whether the national legal system classifies it in that way.[86] It remains to be seen whether the courts will do the same thing and, in particular, to what extent they will apply the concepts of public and private law in deciding what constitutes a civil right.

2.6.3   **Strict limitations to exceptions.** Many Convention rights contain exceptions to the rights. The ECHR has decided that the exceptions are to be applied very strictly. In other words, a narrow interpretation is taken of them.[87]

2.6.4   **Essence of the right.** The ECHR, when considering the impact of the interference by the state in Convention rights, will consider not only

---

[83]   See Reid (1998), page 31 for a fuller list of the principles applied by the ECHR. The ones cited here are thought to be among the most relevant.

[84]   The classic test as is set out in *Associated Provincial Picture Houses Ltd v Wednesbury Corporation* [1948] 1 KB 223.

[85]   See paragraph 3.2.1 of this Guide below.

[86]   See Reid (1998) page 34.

[87]   For example, *Van Mehlen v Netherlands* 23 April 1997, RJD, 1997-111, No. 56, para. 58: limits to defence rights to be "construed very strictly".

whether the particular Article permits that interference, but also what impact it has on the essence of the right.[88]

2.6.5 **The rule of law.** It is a fundamental principle of the Convention that a public body, especially where it is given wide powers, should be subject to some form of effective control over the exercise of that power.[89] In so far as a public authority does interfere with any of the Convention rights, it must always do so lawfully. This means that there must be some form of regulation[90] applied to the body's actions so that what the body may do with its powers is reasonably predictable. In addition, the power to be exercised must be reasonably exercised. It is possible that the exercise of discretion by local authorities in relation to some form of housing matters (e.g. eviction of gypsies/travellers from sites) may not be lawful in this sense.[91]

2.6.6 **Proportionality.** This is an important principle underlying the whole of the Convention. It is particularly relevant to the Articles of the Convention relating to housing issues.[92] The idea of proportionality is that a balance must be struck between the interests of the individual and those of the community. Proportionality examines whether the imposition of a particular measure for the good of the community as a whole (for example, rent controls or compulsory purchase of land for housing) produces an excessive burden on an individual. If it does have a particularly strong effect, the Court will examine what relief has been given to that individual (for example, payment of compensation) as well as the reason for the state action before deciding whether the state's action was proportional to the aims.[93]

2.6.7 **Democratic values.** This includes adoption of a certain tolerance and broadmindedness, and acceptance of a pluralistic society with diverse interests, opinions and lifestyles.[94] State organisations must expect to bear more criticism than others and must act with restraint.[95]

---

[88]   For example *Ashingdane v UK*, 1985 Series A, No. 93, para. 57 (right to marry).
[89]   See, for example, *Silver v UK* 1983 5 EHRR 347, para. 90.
[90]   In the exercise of some powers, such as the provision of housing for rent, this includes the common law, for example landlord and tenant.
[91]   See below at paragraph 4.4.5 of this Guide for more detail.
[92]   See Section 3 of this Guide for more detail.
[93]   For examples of cases where this principle has been applied see: *Sporrong and Lönnroth v Sweden* (1982) 5 EHRR 35 (prevention of full use of house by planning blight for lengthy periods: not proportional); *James v UK* (1986) 8 EHRR 123 (Duke of Westminster's claim that giving his leasehold tenants right to buy the freehold was an unlawful breach of his property rights was rejected: the means were proportional and in the public interest).
[94]   See *Dudgeon* (noted below) at para. 53.
[95]   e.g. *Castells v Spain* [1992] 14 EHRR 445 at paragraph 46.

2.6.8 **The Convention is a "living" document.** It is living in the sense that as the mores of society change, so does the Court's interpretation of the Convention. Changed attitudes to issues such as homosexuality, legitimacy of children, sexual equality etc. have all produced effects in the Court's interpretation of the Convention.[96] The contents of domestic and constitutional law, Council of Europe texts, European law, other international treaties and texts, the human rights law of other countries (such as Canada) may all be of relevance in establishing trends, developments and established principles.[97] If this principle is to be accepted by the courts, a further difficulty in interpretation of the Act is produced. Since the Convention is a living document, its meaning may always change. And that change will only ever occur in the context of a particular case. So, the courts determine the meaning of the Convention. As a result decisions of the ECHR may not always be a reliable guide to the Conventions current meaning, the older the decision the less reliable it is likely to be.[98] Thus, as compared with legislation where change is signalled in advance, the greater fluidity of Convention law will result in the need for greater nimbleness in applying the Convention to policies, practices and rules. Further, the possible use, not only of domestic law, but law from a number of other countries and sources, may make the exact interpretation of any Convention right very difficult.[99]

---

[96]   e.g. *Dudgeon v UK* (1981) 4 EHRR 149 (removal of criminal prohibition on homosexuality); *Johnston v Ireland* (1986) 9 EHRR 203 (illegitimate children's status); Contrast with: *X, Y and Z v UK* (1997) 24 EHRR 143 (status of child brought up by gender change father: no common ground in Europe).

[97]   See Reid (1998), page 39.

[98]   For example, see Section 4.13 of this Guide below for the position on succession by same sex partners.

[99]   See Section 1.8 of this Guide for advice on how to prepare for the Act.

3: PUBLIC HOUSING PROVIDERS – THE KEY CONVENTION RIGHTS

3.1   Four Articles in particular are of direct relevance to housing law issues. Those Articles and their meaning are considered below. The full text of each Article can be found at the end of this Guide. Further understanding of the meaning of the Article, particularly with regard to whom the Articles affect (Sections 1.2, 2.1, 2.4) and the way in which the courts are likely to interpret them (Section 2.6), can be found above.

3.2   **Article 6: Right to fair hearing in connection with civil rights and obligations & minimum rights for criminal trials.**

The following are some of the key elements.

3.2.1   **Civil rights and obligations**. A civil right is one that is a private right as opposed to a public law right. Examples are as follows:

> The right to practise a profession,[100] withdrawal of a licence to sell alcohol,[101] refusal of permission to occupy home,[102] planning blight affecting home,[103] access to child in care.[104] In recent years, the ECHR has held that social security benefits are also civil rights.[105] Thus, housing benefit is likely to be a civil right.

Applications by homeless people to a local authority are *not* private law matters in England & Wales.[106] Other housing aspects are dealt with in Section 4 of this Guide.

---

[100] *H v Belgium* (1987) 10 EHRR 339.
[101] *Tre Traktörer Aktiebolag v Sweden* (1989) 13 EHRR 309.
[102] *Gillow v UK* (1986) 11 EHRR 335.
[103] *Sporrong*, note 93 above.
[104] *Olsson v Sweden (no. 2)* (1992) 17 EHRR 134.
[105] Both benefits based on (national) insurance contributions *Feeldbrugge v The Netherlands* (1986) 8 EHRR 425; and other welfare benefits *Salesi v Italy* (1993) Series A, No. 257-E; and *Schuler-Zgraggen v Switzerland* (1993) 16 EHRR 405.
[106] See *Cocks v Thanet District Council*, note 56 above; also paragraphs 2.6.2 and 4.3.3 of this Guide.

3.2.2 **What is a fair hearing?**[107] There are a number of requirements, all of which are familiar and known in the UK as aspects of natural justice:

- There must be "equality of arms": that is, each party has an opportunity to present their case to the tribunal or court without any substantial disadvantage as regards the opposing party.
- There must be a judicial process, which gives each side a full opportunity of commenting on submissions, and evidence put by the other side.[108]
- There must be a reasoned decision given in public.
- In addition, there are a number of requirements which are specifically included in the text of Article 6 itself.

3.2.3 **Right of access to a court.** Article 6 is not free-standing. It does not by itself guarantee any particular content to the law. Article 6 cannot be used to claim the existence of a right which does not already exist in domestic law.

- If a person can establish that there is a dispute over what can properly be characterised as a "civil right" or obligation, s/he is entitled to access to a court or tribunal to have the claim determined.[109]
- If there is no such right, Article 6 does not apply.[110]
- In some circumstances, this right may require legal aid to be granted to pay for legal representation.[111]

3.2.4 **"Independent and impartial tribunal established by law".** Tribunal includes a court, which must be established by law. The tribunal must be independent from the Government, Parliament and all those appearing before it. The manner of the appointment of the tribunal members and their tenure must demonstrate formal independence.[112] Former Housing Benefit Review Boards would not therefore have complied with Article 6.[113] Semi-formal administrative bodies may be tribunals for this purpose.[114] However, the judicial process has to be seen as a whole.

---

[107] See generally Baker (1998), page 358, and cases cited there.
[108] See *Bates* note 192 below.
[109] See *James*, note 93 above.
[110] See, for example, *Powell and Rayner v UK* (1990) 12 EHRR 355, homeowners living below a flightpath at Heathrow airport complained about excessive noise. The Civil Aviation Act 1982 limits liability for damages for noise caused to homeowners. It was held that therefore there was no "civil right", the determination of which was protected by Article 6. (The court then went on to consider the application on other grounds including Article 1 of the First Protocol: see Section 3.5 of this Guide below).
[111] *Airey v Ireland* (1979) 2 EHRR 305.
[112] *Starrs and Chalmers v Ruxton* note 173 below (the temporary sheriffs case); *Campbell and Fell v UK* (1984) 7 EHRR 165; *Findlay v UK* (1997) 24 EHRR 227; *Coyne v UK* RJD 1997-V 1842.
[113] See Section 4.6 of this Guide. From 2 July 2000 (social security) Appeals Tribunals took over the functions of HBRBs.
[114] E.g. the Board of Prison Visitors: *Campbell and Fell v UK* above.

If a decision is made by a tribunal which does not meet the Article 6 test, an appeal to a court or tribunal that does meet the test may "cure" the defect.[115] The existence of judicial review may or may not cure the defects in any decision made by a housing body which does not meet the Article 6 criteria.[116]

3.2.5 **How the ECHR deals with questions under Article 6 relating to civil matters.** Understanding the way that the ECHR approaches questions arising under Article 6 may be of some help where a housing organisation is faced with a novel question. As a general approach, the ECHR will ask the following questions in all cases, in addition to specific questions relating to the particular facts of the case:

- Is the obligation or right "civil" ("private" as opposed to "public")? If not, Article 6 doesn't apply.
- Is there a genuine and serious dispute about the right or obligation? If not, Article 6 doesn't apply.
- Do the proceedings concern a right or obligation recognised in law? If not, Article 6 doesn't apply.
- Have the guarantees in Article 6(1) been complied with? If so, Article 6 is satisfied.

3.2.6 **Minimum rights in respect of criminal trials.** Occasionally the work of housing professionals brings them into contact with the criminal law. Examples may include:

- environmental protection;
- anti-social behaviour;
- protection from eviction;
- housing benefit fraud.

---

[115] This is a whole field in itself. There are a number of cases that go both ways. See Baker (1998) at pages 71, 123, 276 and 287 and notes 116 &194.

[116] See generally Clyde and Edwards (2000). Some have argued that it is doubtful whether the existence of judicial review can ever "cure" a defective decision where that original decision is one that depended on its findings in relation to disputed facts since it is not the function of the court in a judicial review to review the facts decided upon by the lower tribunal. However, see *R (on the application of Johns & McLellan) v Bracknell Forest District Council* [2001] 33 HLR 45, here judicial review was found to be sufficient to remedy a statutory internal review procedure which it was accepted did not meet the standard of independence and impartiality. The case concerned whether the use of, and procedure for, the recovery of introductory tenancies under the Housing Act 1996, part V, complied with the Convention. Judicial review was found to be sufficient in this case because the decision of the council could be quashed if they either: acted on no evidence at all; reached an unreasonable conclusion from the evidence; failed to take into account relevant considerations or took into account irrelevant ones. Contrast with *Alconbury* (see note 199) where the decision taker was also the policy maker.

In addition to the rights to a fair hearing for civil rights and obligations, those charged with criminal offences are entitled to additional safeguards and strict standards of conduct during the trial. These safeguards are detailed in paragraphs 2 and 3 of the Article, see full text of Article 6 in Appendix 1 of this Guide.

3.3 **Article 8: Right to respect for private and family life, the home and correspondence.**

This Article contains a number of rights. There is little room in this Guide to explore the meaning of the whole Article. Reference should be made to any number of texts for a fuller explanation.[117] The Article inter-reacts with other Articles.[118] The next few paragraphs focus on those aspects which are most concerned with housing issues.

3.3.1 **"Respect for…".** Whenever a public authority makes a decision which affects a person's private or public life etc., it must demonstrate that in making its decision there has been a reasonable balancing between the rights of the individual on the one hand, and the competing interests of the wider community on the other.

3.3.2 **"Family life".**[119] "Family" is given a wider interpretation. It goes beyond marriage and the parent/child relationship to include other relationships demonstrating a sufficiently close personal link between the parties.[120] A family includes relationships between brothers and sisters, nephew and uncle, cohabitees etc.[121] Under ECHR law, a family now includes homosexual relationships.[122] This fits with English law where, at least as far as succession to a regulated tenancy is concerned, homosexual relationships can now fall under the definition of "family".[123] The position of a transsexual may also fall within the definition of "family".[124]

---

[117] For example, Lester and Pannick (1999), pages 165-190; Reid (1998), pages 256, 289, 323, 385; Baker (1998), pages 71-77 and Chapter 6; Supperstone et al. (1999), Chapter 5.

[118] Including 9 (freedom of thought etc.), 10 (freedom of expression), Articles 1 and 2 of the First Protocol (right to property and right to education).

[119] See for a fuller discussion J. Liddy: *The Concept of Family Life under the ECHR* [1998] EHRR 15; Baker (1998) pages 220, 271.

[120] See *Marckx v Belgium* (1979) 2 EHRR 330, (state duty to allow integration of illegitimate children); *Johnston v Ireland* (1986) 9 EHRR 203 (no right to divorce but illegitimate child entitled to protection of rights).

[121] See Lester and Oliver (1997), page 164 for fuller list and the authorities.

[122] *Da Silva Mouta v Portugal*, ECHR, 21 December 1999 see note 249.

[123] *Fitzpatrick v Sterling Housing Association*, paragraph 4.13.2 of this Guide (homosexual partner can succeed to tenancy of partner).

[124] *X, Y and Z v UK* (1997) 24 EHRR 143.

The right to respect for family life does not require the state to make national laws enabling all families to have a home.[125] The Convention is, however, a living instrument and it is not inconceivable that this position might change sometime in the future.

3.3.3 **"Private life"**. Again, "private life" is given a wide definition. It includes to a degree the right to develop and establish relationships (including sexual relationships, whether homosexual or heterosexual) with others for the development and fulfilment of the person's personality.[126] The effect of serious pollution has been held to amount to an invasion of private life,[127] as has substantial noise nuisance.[128] It is not an interference with private life to refuse a tenant permission to have a pet.[129] The collection of information about an individual can amount to an interference with private life.[130]

3.3.4 **"Home"**. "Home" is given a fairly wide meaning. It does not necessarily have to be the place where the person is presently living.

- Some degree of permanence or attachment is necessary.[131]
- The right to respect for one's home includes the right to live in it and not to be evicted except by lawful process.[132]
- A compulsory purchase order may interfere with this right.[133]

---

[125] *Barreto v Portugal* A 334 (1992) (ECHR). This might seem surprising but it should be remembered that the purpose of the Convention is not to provide citizens with economic and social rights, but rather to provide minimum civil and political rights which protect the individual from exercise of arbitrary power by the state, for example, from the arbitrary confiscation of property. In this sense it is logical that the Convention should protect citizens with existing legal rights from unwarranted interference by the state rather than create new economic or social rights for those at present who have none.

[126] *Dudgeon v UK* (1981) 4 EHRR 149 (criminalisation of homosexual activities unlawful as interfering with private life); *Neimietz v Germany* (1992) 16 EHRR 97 (search of lawyer's office interfered with private and home life).

[127] *Lopez-Ostra v Spain* (1995) 20 EHRR 277.

[128] *Rayner v UK* (1986) 47 DR 5 and *Powell and Rayner v UK* (1990) 12 EHRR 355 (aircraft noise from Heathrow airport).

[129] *X v Iceland* (1976) 5 DR 86 (in this case, a dog; the tenancy agreement forbade it).

[130] For example, in a census, by way of fingerprinting, or maintaining medical records. However, the public authority in such cases will usually be able to justify that infringement under one of the exceptions in Article 8(2). Note also that the Data Protection Act 1998 provides for substantial protection in this respect: see Section 4.15 of this Guide below. Unlawful disclosure of information gathered will usually amount to a breach of Article 8.

[131] The precise facts are important. See *Gillow v UK* (1986) 11 EHRR 97 (right to reside in house in Guernsey upheld). Contrast with *Loizidou v Turkey* (1995) 20 EHRR 99 (land which the applicant had in northern Cyprus on which the applicant had intended to build an apartment block including a flat for her family was not a "home"). See also Harris et al. (1996), page 317.

[132] *Wiggins v UK* (1978) 13 DR 40; *Howard v UK* (1987) 52 DR 198.

[133] *Howard v UK* (1987) 52 DR 198.

- It includes the right to peaceful enjoyment of the home.[134]
- It does not give the right to have a home.[135]
- Home can include land owned by a traveller on which the traveller wants to site his/her caravan.[136]
- There is no right to choose the most suitable place to live in so as to develop family life.[137]
- If the applicant has no legal right to the home, it may be that the applicant cannot rely on this Article.[138]

3.3.5 **Justification of interference.** Article 8, like several other Articles, permits interference with the rights under certain circumstances. These are where the public authority can show that the interference is as follows:

- "In accordance with the law[139]
- **and** is **necessary**[140] in a democratic society in the interests of
  - national security, **or**
  - public safety, **or**
  - the economic well-being of the country, **or**
  - for the prevention of disorder or crime, **or**
  - for the protection of health or morals, **or**
  - for the protection of the rights and freedoms of others".

---

[134] *Lopez-Ostra v Spain*, above (pollution); *Arondelle v UK* (1982) 26 DR 5 (house near Gatwick airport, unable to sell and denied planning permission for change of use: case settled by the UK).

[135] *X v Federal Republic of Germany* (1956) 1 YB 202.

[136] *Buckley v UK* (1994) 18 EHRR CD 123 (where it was held that, although the refusal of permission to the traveller/gypsy to site the caravan on her own land was an interference with her right to respect for her home, that interference was justified in the public interest). See also *Burton v UK* [1996] 22 EHRR CD 135 where a gypsy, unable to find a permanent site for her caravan, failed in her attempt to prove a breach of Articles 8 and 14 against the local authority. There have been a large number of decisions involving travellers/gypsies and the siting of caravans. See Harris, O'Boyle and Warbrick (1995) at page 319. See also Supperstone et al. (1999), *Local Authorities and the Human Rights Act 1998*, pages 113-116.

[137] *Ahmut v Netherlands* (1996) 24 EHRR 62 (Moroccan national refused residence permit in Netherlands for his son); *Gul v Switzerland* (1996) 22 EHRR 93.

[138] In *S v UK* (1986) 47 DR 274, who was the appellant in *Harrogate BC v Simpson*, (note 244 below) the Commission decided that a lesbian who was refused permission to succeed to her late partner's council tenancy had not had her Convention rights interfered with on the grounds, among others, that she never had a legal right to the tenancy, the contractual relationship having been between her late partner and the landlord. It must now be doubted whether that decision would still be applied today. See also paragraph 4.13.2 of this Guide.

[139] Lawfulness presupposes compliance with the domestic law but also requires conformity with the aims and purposes of the Convention which embodies the principle of the rule of law in a wider sense.

[140] And, ECHR caselaw shows, proportionate to the aim sought to be achieved.

So, not every interference will be unlawful. In addition, the principles of interpretation of Convention rights come into play which may allow a wide degree of discretion to the public authority: see Section 2.6 above.[141]

The justification can only be invoked where the interference has been "in accordance with the law". This means that the measures taken by the public authority must be in terms of some rule of law which is established, the terms of which were reasonably accessible to the applicant and which is formulated with "sufficient precision to enable the citizen to regulate his conduct".[142] Thus, if a public authority, such as a housing department, makes a decision affecting a tenant's home, private or family life, it must be in accordance with publicly available rules (which includes common law, statute, regulations, or DTLR guidance) which are formulated with sufficient precision. Totally unfettered discretion is likely to be unlawful.

"Necessary" is neither synonymous with "indispensable", nor does it have the flexibility of expressions such as "admissible, ordinary, useful, reasonable or desirable".[143] Its meaning falls somewhere between these extremes.

It is for the public authority to satisfy the court that one of the grounds for the exceptions is satisfied. If and when the applicant shows a breach of Article 8(1), the onus is then on the public authority to show which of the exceptions are satisfied and why. The court then weighs up the competing considerations, for the applicant on the one hand and the public authority on the other, in the light of the exceptions in the Article and the principles of interpretation (see above). For this reason, it may be difficult in any one case to predict what the decision of the court would be.

3.3.6   **How the ECHR deals with questions under Article 8.**[144] Understanding the way that the ECHR approaches questions arising under Article 8 may be of some help where a housing organisation is faced with a novel question. As a general approach, the ECHR will ask the following

---

141   See, for example, *Howard v UK* (1985) 52 DR 198, where the Commission found no breach of Article 8 in a compulsory purchase case since, although there was an interference of Article 8, the procedures were fair, compensation was given, there was a fair planning enquiry and the purpose of the compulsory purchase was for legitimate ends.

142   *Sunday Times v UK* (1979) 2 EHRR 245 at para. 49. In *Silver v UK* (1983) 5 EHRR 347, the ECHR held that instructions issued by the Home Office to prison governors regarding treatment of prisoners which were not published could not be "law" and therefore decisions based on these instructions could not be in accordance with the law so far as they were not known or accessible.

143   Baker (1998), page 75.

144   This is adapted from Reid (1998), page 41.

questions in all cases, in addition to specific questions relating to the particular facts of the case:

- Does the complaint concern the right to respect for family, private life, the home or correspondence (i.e. Article 8(1))? If not, Article 8 does not apply.
- Is there an interference with that right? If not, Article 8 does not apply.

As regards justification:

- Is the interference lawful? If not, interference cannot be justified.
- Is there a legitimate aim? If not, interference cannot be justified.
- Is the interference "necessary" (taking into account notions such as "pressing social need, margin of appreciation, proportionality, procedural safeguards and relevant and sufficient reason)? If not, interference cannot be justified.
- If the complainer is claiming that a positive right exists (e.g. that the local authority has a duty to take action to stop an anti-social neighbour), does that positive right exist taking into account proportionality, the aim of the Article and any other relevant facts? If not, Article 8 has not been violated.

3.4   Article 14: Prohibition of discrimination.

It is often thought that this Article bans discrimination by public authorities against people in all circumstances. It does not. It reads as follows:

> The enjoyment of the **rights and freedoms set forth in this Convention** shall be secured without discrimination on any ground such as sex, race, colour, language, religion, political or other opinion, national or social origin, association with a national minority, property, birth or other status.

So, this Article is subsidiary to other Articles. It is not a "stand-alone" Article. Before it can be invoked, it is necessary first to identify another Convention right to which the applicant can claim s/he is entitled, and then show that his/her Convention rights, in terms of that Article have been violated, *and* that the reason for the violation is discrimination on some ground or other. It is as though it were an integral part of each of the other Articles which confer substantive rights.[145] The discrimination must be on the grounds of some "status" or other: the Article itself only gives some examples of status.

---

[145]   See the *Belgian Linguistics case* (1968) 1 EHRR 252.

3.4.1 **Comparator.** The person claiming discrimination must show that others in an analogous situation are treated differently. Like must be compared with like. For example, comparison of a married couple with a cohabiting couple is not comparison of like with like, as the married couple have deliberately chosen a different status from the unmarried couple, which carries with it, legitimately, a different corpus of rights and obligations.[146] The fact that English law and Scottish law may treat a person differently in similar circumstances is not differential treatment on the ground of status.[147] Differences in the law between England and Wales are likely to become significant over time as the National Assembly makes full use of its regulation-making powers.

3.4.2 **Justification.** Furthermore, the caselaw has established that, even where relevant discrimination is established, the state may be permitted to justify the discrimination on reasonable and objective grounds, having regard also to the "margin of appreciation".[148] The discrimination must pursue some legitimate aim and the means employed must be proportional to the objective it is intended to meet.[149] The cases show that this test has been satisfied for reasons such as:

- The protection of the family.[150]
- The protection of the health of children.[151]
- The giving of preferential treatment for housing to those with a strong attachment to an area.[152]
- The enfranchisement of leaseholders.[153]
- The suspension of eviction orders at a time of acute housing shortage.[154]

The effect of the discrimination must be "proportional" to the desired aim.

---

[146] According to *Lindsay and Lindsay v UK* (1986) 49 DR 181 (taxation of unmarried couples).

[147] See App. No. 13473/87 (Dec.) 11 July 1988 (poll tax being applied in Scotland before England); *Nelson v UK* (1986) 49 DR 181 (Scottish juvenile offender entitled to less remission than an English offender).

[148] This is so despite the apparently absolute and unqualified terms of the Article. See paragraph 2.6.1 of this Guide above for the meaning of margin of appreciation. See also Reid (1998), pages 194-200.

[149] See *Larkos v Cyprus* (1999) 7 BHRC 244. The only ECHR case where a tenant has successfully challenged a possession order. Under Cypriot law a tenant was excluded from security of tenure granted to private sector tenants by virtue of the fact that they were a tenant of the government. The exclusion could not be justified because the government rented the property to him in a private law capacity. His position was sufficiently similar to that of other private tenants.

[150] *S v UK* (1986) 47 DR 274.

[151] *Hoffman v Austria* (1993) 17 EHRR 293 (Jehovah Witnesses).

[152] *Gillow v UK* (1986) 11 EHRR 335 (Guernsey housing case).

[153] *James* (note 93 above).

[154] *Spadea v Italy* (1995) 21 EHRR 482.

3.4.3   **Direct and indirect discrimination.**[155] The Convention caselaw shows that justification of discrimination is possible even where the discrimination is direct (e.g. women tenants only) as opposed to indirect (e.g. all applicants must be six foot tall, a requirement that is applied to all but which fewer women than men can satisfy). The position is different in UK law.[156]

3.4.4   **How the ECHR deals with questions under Article 14.**[157] Understanding the way that the ECHR approaches questions arising under Article 14 may be of some help where a housing organisation is faced with a novel question. As a general approach, the ECHR will ask the following questions in all cases in addition to specific questions relating to the particular facts of the case:

- Is there another Convention right in question? If not, Article 14 doesn't apply.
- Is there a difference in treatment? If not, Article 14 doesn't apply.
- Is the difference in treatment between people in sufficiently similar situations? If not, Article 14 doesn't apply.
- Is the difference because of "status"? If not, Article 14 doesn't apply.
- Is the different treatment justified on objective and reasonable grounds (including consideration of reasonable aims, proportionality and margin of appreciation)? If so, there is no violation of Article 14. If the treatment is not justifiable, there is a violation.

3.5   **Protocol 1, Article 1: Protection of property.**

The purpose of this Article is to protect rights in relation to property, or possessions as it is referred to in the Convention. The Article says that:

> Every natural or legal person is entitled to the peaceful enjoyment of his possessions. No one shall be deprived of his possessions except in the public interest and subject to the conditions provided for by law and by the general principles of international law. The preceding provisions shall not, however, in any way impair the right of a State to enforce such laws as it deems necessary to control the use of property in accordance with the general interest or to secure the payment of taxes or other contributions or penalties.

---

[155]   It is not yet clear whether the ECHR explicitly recognises this distinction. However, it is a distinction now well known to UK law and it is thought that the UK courts, in interpreting Convention rights, would take note of this distinction.

[156]   Another example of how the rights currently enjoyed by those in the UK are superior to those minimum standards guaranteed by the Convention. Under both the Sex Discrimination Act 1975 and the Race Relations Act 1976, direct discrimination can never be justified. However, the ECHR have said that "particularly weighty grounds" would have to be adduced to justify discrimination because of sex. The position is different under the Disability Discrimination Act 1995. There are no laws in the UK, however, prohibiting discrimination on other grounds, such as age. Positive discrimination is permissible potentially under Article 14.

[157]   The text following is adapted from Reid (1998), page 41.

The Article can be invoked where an owner's enjoyment of their property is restricted or interfered with. Therefore "victims" here could potentially include RSLs and private landlords, as well as individuals. This can result in a tension between the property interests of corporate bodies and the social and economic interests of individual vulnerable tenants who might expect the state to legislate to protect them. Generally the approach of the ECHR to this conflict is to give the state a wide margin of appreciation.[158]

3.5.1 **What are possessions?** The definition is very wide. It includes:

- All forms of legal interest in land such as:
  - Outright ownership.
  - Leases and tenancy agreements.[159]
  - Licences to occupy (such as some hostel dwellers).[160]
- By extension it may also include the right to buy enjoyed by secure and some assured tenants.[161]
- It applies to possessions held by individuals and organisations.[162]
- There must be a pre-existing right under national law to be protected.[163]

3.5.2 **What is "deprivation"?** This includes:

- Complete dispossession (such as eviction or compulsory purchase).[164]
- Partial reduction in rights such as use.[165]
- Challenges to rent controls have been the subject of some cases.[166]

---

[158] See, for example, *Mellacher, Spadea* and *Velosa Barretto v Portugal* (1995). All these cases concerned various landlord challenges to security of tenure and rent control legislation, all the challenges failed because the laws came within the states margin of appreciation.

[159] *Mellacher v Austria* (1989) 12 EHRR 391 (landlord and rent controls); *Iatridis v Greece*, unreported, 25 March 1999, ECHR.

[160] By parity of reasoning with *A, B and Company AS v FRG* (1978) 14 DR 146 which held that contractual rights may be "possessions".

[161] Housing Act 1985, Part V.

[162] As in the *James* case, note 93 above.

[163] See App. No. 19217/91 (Dec.) 21 January 1994, 76-A DR, the right to live in a property of which one was not an owner (where the dispute was over succession) was not a possession.

[164] See *Howard v UK* (1985) 52 DR 198 (compulsory purchase of house and land under powers in the Town Planning Acts).

[165] As in *James* above.

[166] Rent control is control of property rather than deprivation, see for example in *Mellacher v Austria*, above, where rent reductions of up to 79% were not a violation of the right to property. See also App. No. 15434 (Dec.), 15 Feb 1990, 64 DR 232, where a landlord, affected by a House of Lords decision to do with "sham" licences (thus bringing his licensed properties under the Rent Control regime) was unsuccessful in his ECHR challenge despite losing up to £45 per property per week.

- Legislation restricting recovery of possession or prohibiting eviction has been the subject of some cases.[167]

3.5.3 **When can interference be justified?** As with many of the other Articles, the state can justify interference with property rights in some circumstances.

- The pursuit of legitimate social and economic policies and the implementation of social justice may amount to legitimate interference.[168]
- Where a public authority is exercising such powers in accordance with the law, it is unlikely that the courts will be quick to interfere with any such appropriation of individual property.
- Legitimate social and economic aims to make accommodation more affordable justified rent controls.
- The court will look to see whether the public authority struck a fair balance between the rights of the individual property owner and the rights of the community in any expropriation of the property.
- A significant factor in any such balance will be the availability of compensation, reflecting the value of the property expropriated.[169]

3.5.4 **How the ECHR deals with questions under Article 1 of the First Protocol.**[170]

Understanding the way that the ECHR approaches questions arising under this Article may be of some help where a housing organisation is faced with a novel question. As a general approach, the ECHR will ask the following questions in all cases, in addition to specific questions relating to the particular facts of the case:

---

[167] *Spadea and Scalabrino v Italy* (1995) 21 EHRR 482 (suspension of court decrees for eviction at the end of lease as a result of government legislation was permissible as there was a genuine social need (lack of housing) and the landlord was still free to receive rent and sell property). In *Scollo v Italy* (1995) 22 EHRR 514, the landlord was unemployed, disabled and needed his flat for himself but was prevented from gaining possession by a combination of the same legislation as in *Spadea* and bureaucratic ineptitude. It was held that he ought to have been entitled to repossession of the flat, in the circumstances (and sooner than the 11 years it took him!). Similarly in *Immobilare Saffri v Italy* (2000) 30 EHRR 756, Italian law which phased evictions was found not to be in breach of the Article because it was in the public interest. However, any actual interference must be both proportional and not impact in an arbitrary or unforeseeable manner. On the facts the interference was not proportional because the landlord had been kept in suspense for six years without any indication when the position would change. See also *AO v Italy* App. No. 22534/93.

[168] As in *James v UK, Spadea v Italy* and *Mellacher v Austria*, above.

[169] *Howard v UK*, note 141 above.

[170] The following is adapted from Reid (1998) page 41.

- Does the case involve "possessions"? If not, the Article does not apply.
- Does the act or omission complained of amount to a deprivation, a control of use or an interference with peaceful enjoyment? If not, the Article does not apply.
- In considering whether the interference was justified, the Court will ask:
  - Did the interference have a legitimate aim (in the general or public sense)?
  - Was the act or omission lawful?
  - Was the matter within the margin of appreciation?[171]
  - Was the exercise of the authority's power proportional (including procedural safeguards and compensation)?

---

171   The ECHR has always given member states a wide margin of appreciation in such cases: *James,* note 93 above.

4: Human Rights and Housing Issues

4.1   **Introduction.** The purpose of this Section of the Guide is to look at a number of particular housing management issues in the light of the Act. It will not be necessary to have read the preceding three Sections to make sense of this Section. Reference, however, will be made to concepts, principles and ideas that have been explained in the earlier Sections. Paragraph 1.8.3 above contains recommendations about how to conduct a human rights audit. It is not possible at this stage to predict precisely what the courts will do with the Act. The courts are not bound by ECHR law: they only have to take it into account. It may be that some judges will take a rather narrow view of the Act and this seems to be the position taken in England,[172] whereas in Scotland the early experience was somewhat different where the courts did not shy away from taking a broader and interventionist view.[173] All that can be done here, therefore, is to examine particular housing issues that may raise a Convention point and to suggest whether a challenge on Convention grounds might be successful.[174] The Articles of the Convention that are relevant to each issue are specified at the beginning of each section. Full reference to caselaw and other authorities is given in Section 3 above.

4.1.1   In summary, the following is suggested as a general approach where a particular issue is being considered by the public housing provider:

- Is the act or omission complained of one by a local authority, a Government department or an RSL exercising a public function? If not, no Convention issue arises.
- Is the person challenging it a victim of the act or omission? If not, no Convention issue arises (at that point anyway).
- Does, or would, the act or omission violate a Convention right?

---

172   For example, *McCann* and *Johns* see note 44 and Sections 4.5 and 4.9 of this Guide.

173   *Starrs and Chalmers v Ruxton* 2000 JC 208, above (the temporary sheriffs decision); *Robb v HMA* 18 March 2000 (Article 6: trial within a reasonable time); *Geoffrey, Ptr* 16 March 2000 (Art. 5, reasons for opposing bail must be given); *Brown v Ruxton* 4 February 2000 (drunk driving accused cannot be forced to self-incriminate).

174   The tenant or applicant may also have rights or remedies under English law even if the 1998 Act does not apply (and additionally if it does apply).

If so, which one(s)? The answer will involve examining the right in question, the caselaw, interpretation rules (e.g. proportionality), and any exceptions contained within the Convention (e.g. "necessary in a democratic society..."). If there is no violation of a specified Convention right, there is no Convention issue.

- If there would be a violation, can the public authority act otherwise by interpreting any relevant primary legislation in a way compatible with the Convention? If so, it must do so.
- If there would be a violation and that is caused only by a common law rule, that rule must be ignored and the Act applied.
- If the public authority cannot interpret primary legislation (e.g. an Act of Parliament) to avoid conflict with the Convention, the public authority must follow the legislation. It will be for the courts to make a declaration of incompatibility. If the legislation is secondary (such as a regulation made by the Secretary of State in England or the National Assembly in Wales),[175] the LA must ignore it if there would otherwise be a violation of a Convention right.[176]

4.2 **Allocation of housing.** *Articles 8 and 14.*

4.2.1 Since the Convention does not guarantee a right to housing, no Convention rights issue will arise from the mere fact that an applicant is refused a house. However, following *Donoghue*,[177] the letting of houses by a public authority is almost certainly a public function. So the lettings or allocation policies on which an individual decision is based will require to conform to the Convention: and Article 8 in particular. Therefore allocation policies will need to be scrutinised to ensure that "respect" for an applicant's private and family life is given. Some allocation policies may already incidentally do this since assessment of need will depend at least partially on the size of the family and the current living conditions of the applicant. Such allocation policies may give rise to legitimate expectations on the part of applicants for housing that such policies will be applied by the housing provider.[178]

4.2.2 If an applicant family is banned from the housing list (for example, for anti-social behaviour), there is a potential violation of the respect for

---

[175] In Scotland all Acts of the Scottish Parliament are secondary legislation and so can be directly challenged by judicial intervention in the same way as regulations in England and Wales. See note 80 above.

[176] Unless the primary legislation explicitly prevents this.

[177] *Donoghue v Poplar HARCA* [2001] EWCA Civ 595.

[178] The legitimate expectation will be to do not only with procedural matters (how things are done), but also, arguably, with substantive matters (the content of rights): see Clyde and Edwards (2000), paras. 19.16 to 19.25 for discussion.

family life, depending on the effect that that ban has. However, the housing provider may be able to rely on the exceptions in Article 8(2), for example if it can show that the ban is "necessary...for public safety or...for the protection of the rights and freedoms of others". Bans from housing lists are more frequently made because of previous or existing rent arrears. It is a little more difficult to see how the Article 8(2) exceptions can apply. The most obvious one is "...for the protection of the rights and freedoms of others...". The argument might be that if prior rent arrears are not taken into account, global rent arrears may rise, causing an increase in rent or decrease in the quality of housing conditions generally.

4.2.3   So, in all cases, before banning someone from allocation of housing, on whatever ground, the housing provider must be able to show that it has taken into account the Convention rights. Where it proposes to make a decision that will, or may, affect that applicant's Convention rights, it should have sound, well-grounded and well-documented reasons for doing so. The decision must also be "proportional". Thus, a lifetime ban is unlikely to be "proportional". A regular review or a limit on the period of the ban will be necessary. Also necessary will be an investigation into the reasons for the circumstances. So, if the reason is rent arrears, the housing provider will require at the very least to have investigated the reasons for the rent arrears, the effect that the ban would have and to weigh that factor in with other factors before making its decision.

4.2.4   It should also be noted that in order for the housing authority to avail itself of one of the Article 8(2) exceptions, it must show that that breach is "in accordance with the law and is necessary in a democratic society". Allocation policies are not prescribed by law. Rather, there is an obligation for local authorities and RSLs to have allocation policies and to publish them.[179] Local authorities have an additional duty which is to give "reasonable preference" to certain applicants.[180] It is unclear whether a decision made in accordance with a published allocations policy is one made "in accordance with the law". At the very least, a housing provider that makes a decision on allocations which is challenged under the Act will have to show that it did so in accordance with that policy (rather than some informal understanding or bureaucratic decision) and can demonstrate that, with proper records displaying a rational decision-making process.[181]

---

[179]   Housing Act 1996, Sections 167 & 168. For RSLs the requirement is set out in guidance (known as performance standards) issued by the Housing Corporation/National Assembly. For power to issue guidance see Housing Act 1996, section 36.

[180]   Housing Act 1996, Section 168(2).

[181]   See *Gallacher v Stirling Council*, Court of Session, 2 May 2000, L. Macfadyen, for an example of an allocation decision made in accordance with a practice rather than anything in writing.

4.2.5 Article 14 prohibits discrimination (based on a person's "status"), in the implementation of allocation decisions if an Article 8 right is affected. But, by their very nature, allocation decisions and policies are intended to discriminate as between competing applications for (often) limited housing. This is permissible provided that certain conditions are satisfied. See Section 3.4 above. In summary, allocation policies should be scrutinised to ensure that, in so far as they do discriminate between applicants on the grounds of status, that is done within the Convention limits.

4.3 **Homelessness applications.** *Articles 6, 8 and 14.*

4.3.1 Applications made by homeless persons to a local authority under Part VII of the Housing Act 1996 raise similar issues to allocations in the paragraph above, to which reference should also be made. Because the Convention does not guarantee a right to housing, even to those who are homeless, the rights in Part VII are substantially superior to the Convention guarantees. In general terms, the Convention cannot be used in order to widen the content of Part VII (for example, to assert that single persons should be covered by the Act). However, in so far as a person is covered by Part VII, the implementation must be in accordance with the Convention rights.

4.3.2 There is no real minimum standard of housing to be provided under Part VII.[182] The housing provided does not have to be suitable or reasonably suitable for the applicant's needs. If, however, the applicant is in priority need and not intentionally homeless, the duty to secure accommodation may continue if the applicant reasonably refuses accommodation which is suitable for their needs.[183] The applicant can challenge suitability through the review and appeal mechanisms discussed below (paragraph 4.3.3). Despite the right to refuse an offer and request a review the Act does not directly change the position as regards to suitability, as the Convention does not provide minimum guarantees for the quality of public housing stock (see further Section 4.11 below). In so far as the conditions of the housing provided interfere with the privacy or family life of the applicant (for example, some bed and breakfast accommodation or property in severe disrepair), there may be an argument that an Article 8(1) right has been violated or in very extreme cases Article 3, where considering all the circumstances the particular offer would subject the applicant to inhuman

---

[182] Although there is no express provision preventing an authority from meeting its duty using unfit or overcrowded property, they must at least consider their other Housing Act 1985 duties relating to slum clearance, houses in multiple occupation and overcrowding when reaching their decision. See Housing Act 1996, Section 210.

[183] Housing Act 1996, Section 193(7).

or degrading treatment. Furthermore, it is possible that in the future, there will be "leakage" of Convention jurisprudence in the application of domestic legislation so that a local authority being challenged in respect of its refusal to offer only one (allegedly) unsuitable house may have to explain its reasons and show that its action was proportional.

4.3.3 If an applicant has been refused housing under Part VII, there is a right to an internal review and subsequently, where a point of law is in dispute, an appeal to the county court.[184] Ultimately the county court decision will also be subject to judicial review. Will an internal review with appeal rights only on a point of law be sufficient to conform to Article 6(1) (right to a fair and public hearing)? The answer is that Article 6(1) probably does not apply. This is because Article 6 only applies in relation to the determination of "civil rights and obligations": not public law matters (see paragraph 3.2.1 above). The House of Lords has said that local authorities' decisions in relation to applications under the homelessness legislation are not private law matters.[185] Even if the courts do accept that homeless assistance is a civil right then it is likely that the appeal system and the judicial review will be sufficient to save the review process from an Article 6 challenge.[186]

4.4 **Eviction. *Articles 6, 8, 14 and First Protocol, Article 1.***

4.4.1 The decision whether to take legal proceedings to evict a tenant is an aspect of the management of housing stock. Housing management is not an activity which is exclusively confined to the public sphere, so ordinarily on its own is unlikely to be regarded as a "public function" when performed by a hybrid body. This position could, however, be reversed if the decision to evict was directly linked to an activity which is exclusively reserved for the public sphere. For example, housing provided by a hybrid body whilst assisting a local authority with an interim duty to accommodate pending a final homelessness decision.[187] Of course, the Convention will apply to eviction proceedings where the landlord is a pure public body such as a Government department. [188]

---

[184] Housing Act 1996 ss 203-204.

[185] See paragraph 2.6.2 and paragraph 3.2.1 of this Guide above. If, however, courts were to decide otherwise, the next question would be whether the review process followed by appeal on a point of law and then judicial review is a process which conforms to Article 6(1) rights. If the process was found to be inadequate because the various appeal stages (including judicial review) did not allow a full review of the facts, that would of course be a matter for Parliament rather than the local authority. For a discussion as to whether judicial review is sufficient, see notes 116 and 199.

[186] See *Johns* Section 4.5 of this Guide below.

[187] See *Donoghue* paragraph 2.1.2 of this Guide.

[188] See *Johns* (Section 4.5 of this Guide) and *Larkos* (note 149).

If the Convention does not apply there will nevertheless be consequences for the provider because the courts themselves are bound to apply the Convention (see paragraphs 2.1.1 and 2.1.3 above). If the Convention does apply then the housing provider must be able to demonstrate that it has applied the Act to that decision and in particular Articles 8, 14 and Article 1 of the First Protocol. In extreme cases, Article 3 may also be relevant – for example, the decision to evict someone who has a severe disability (especially from adapted accommodation) or someone who is very seriously ill. Thus, at the very least, the internal policies of the housing provider will have to be scrutinised to ensure that consideration is given to these Articles, (as well as other relevant matters) before a decision is made to seek eviction.

4.4.2 There is a further check on the housing provider in that the court is obliged to apply the Convention when making its decisions. Thus, where the court has to consider whether it is reasonable to evict (as it does for most of the grounds usually relied on in secure and assured tenancies), the Convention rights will then enter into the court's consideration at that point. However, in cases where the court does not have discretion (such as where an assured tenant has more than three months' rent arrears)[189] the position is clearer. The restricted role of the courts in action under the mandatory grounds is essentially a legislative policy decision which the courts are likely to accept as necessary to protect the rights and freedoms of others.[190] Whether the restricted role of the court breaches the Convention will depend on the extent to which the restriction is legitimate and proportionate. Following *Donoghue*[191] it seems likely that the court will defer to the will of Parliament as being within the margin of appreciation.

4.4.3 A court hearing, at least where reasonableness can be pled as a defence, will also satisfy Article 6 in respect of the tenant's "civil rights" (the right to occupy the house under the tenancy agreement) and Article 1 of the First Protocol (the right not to be deprived of a "possession" (the tenancy) otherwise than in accordance with the law etc.). On the other hand Article 6 will be breached if the tenant is not given a proper

---

189   For example, ground 8 (three months' rent arrears at the date of the raising of the eviction action and the date of the hearing), to Schedule 5 of the Housing Act 1988 (assured tenancy cases).

190   The obligation on the court in terms of Section 6 (see above at Section 2.5 of this Guide) is only to interpret legislation compatibly with the Convention in so far as it is possible to do so. The court could however, if requested, make a declaration that the 1988 Act is incompatible with the 1998 Act if it was persuaded that the absence of the ability of the court to take into account arguments based on the Convention as a defence to the eviction action was a violation of the tenant's Convention rights.

191   *Donoghue v Poplar HARCA* [2001] EWCA Civ 595.

opportunity to prepare their defence and seek advice and assistance, particularly in cases where skilled representation would be likely to make a real difference to the outcome. For example, possession proceedings for anti-social behaviour where the credibility of witnesses was likely to be a significant factor. [192]

4.4.4   The position of hostel dwellers poses particular difficulties for local authorities. Simply put, occupiers of local authority hostels (who are not tenants) have no lease or tenancy agreement and may be evicted with little or no notice. No court action is required.[193] (The position is different if the hostel dweller is a tenant or if the facts surrounding his/her occupation give rise to the implication of a tenancy.) Although the lack of security provided by the legislation for hostel dwellers may be the subject of a challenge, the courts are likely to consider the reasons why Parliament has chosen to restrict their rights. Provided the restriction is necessary and proportionate, which following *Donoghue*[194] seems likely, the courts will not grant a declaration. Nevertheless although the legislation may be sound, it allows the authority a considerable degree of discretion as to how it should act. The use of the procedure may be disproportionate in individual cases if the authority acts in a particularly arbitrary, oppressive or heavy-handed manner. In such circumstances a number of Convention issues arise. If the hostel is the person's usual residence (many hostel dwellers are long term) then the hostel is a home. Summary eviction may very well fall foul of Article 8 ("...respect for home...private life...and family..."); Article 6 (right to a hearing) and Article 1 to the First Protocol (no arbitrary deprivation of "possessions": i.e. the right to live in the hostel) or in extreme cases Article 3 (prohibition on degrading treatment).

It is strongly suggested that local authorities substantially revise their hostel management policies and, in particular, ensure that no eviction is contemplated without a full, documented examination of all the circumstances. Where there is any doubt as to whether summary eviction would be unlawful, the occupier's agreement or licence to occupy may be terminated and an action for possession raised in the county court. The district judge would decide the case on common-law principles since the defender/occupier does not have an assured or a secure tenancy. The court would be obliged to apply the Convention and would not be

---

[192]   See *Bates v London Borough of Croydon* [2001] EWCA Civ 134, in contrast see *McCann*, note 222 and *Clingham* note 223 below.

[193]   See *Brennan v Lambeth L.B.C* 30 HLR 481, in cases where the occupier is local authority hostel dweller with an excluded licence, Protection from Eviction Act 1977 Section 3A(8)(a) and Housing Act 1985 Section 622.

[194]   *Donoghue v Poplar HARCA* [2001] EWCA Civ 595.

prevented from doing so by "incompatible legislation". Thus, in effect, the defender/occupier in such a case would have a defence to the action if s/he could show that the action amounted to a violation of his/her Convention rights. The usual principles of interpretation of Convention rights of course apply (see Sections 2.5 and 2.6 above).

4.4.5 Similar issues arise in the case of gypsies/travellers in connection with evictions from local authority sites. Once again, the Convention will apply potentially in the case of any proposed eviction or removal from the site. Such a site may well be a home for the purposes of Article 8. There have been some cases in Scotland where local authorities have removed gypsies/travellers from sites and have successfully resisted legal challenge.[195] Such cases may not be decided the same way in the future. Even if the site is not a "home", other aspects of the Convention may apply, for example, Article 3 in extreme cases where on the facts eviction would be particularly inhuman or degrading.[196] There has been a substantial amount of caselaw on the subject of gypsies/travellers, particularly in England. Some cases have been to the ECHR.[197] In *Buckley v UK*[198] the ECHR held that the refusal of a local authority to give a gypsy planning permission to allow her to site her caravan on her own land was not a breach of the Convention. A key issue in this and other cases is that of "proportionality" (see paragraph 2.6.6 above).

4.5 **Introductory tenancies and starter tenancies. *Articles 6, 8 and 14.***

4.5.1 The use of introductory tenancies and the associated streamlined procedure for eviction has already been the subject of a Human Rights Act challenge. The procedures for obtaining possession of an introductory tenancy are set out in the Housing Act 1996. The procedure starts with the service of a notice on the tenant that possession is being sought in the courts. The tenant has a statutory right to an internal review provided they request one within the 14 day time limit. If the tenant requests a review the local authority is obliged to conduct one and cannot proceed with possession until it has been completed. The review directly determines the authorities right to obtain possession so Article 6 is engaged. However, although an internal review does not meet the standards of independence and impartiality required by Article 6, the right to judicial review in this

---

[195] See, for example, *McPhee v North Lanarkshire Council* 1998 SLT 1317 and *Stewart v Inverness District Council* 1992 SLT 690.
[196] An Article 3 challenge was considered in *Buckley v UK* (1996) 23 EHRR 101, the challenge failed but only because on the particular facts her suffering did not reach the minimum level of severity.
[197] See *X v FRG* note 135 above.
[198] *Buckley v UK* (1996) 23 EHRR 101.

case has been found to be sufficient.[199] The statutory *procedure* therefore conforms with the Convention but this still leaves open the possibility that its *use* may be disproportionate and therefore be open to an Article 8 challenge on the particular facts of the case.

4.5.2 Does the use of introductory tenancies interfere with the right to respect for the home under Article 8 of the Convention? The eviction process will certainly engage Article 8 and therefore by implication the use of the introductory tenancy regime will interfere with the right to respect for the home. [200] The question is therefore whether the interference is within the margin of appreciation allowed by Article 8. There is no doubt that the scheme being statutory is in accordance with the law. Whether the interference is justified therefore depends on whether the interference is necessary for the protection of the rights and freedoms of others. The courts have taken the view that the scheme is both "necessary" and proportionate. There is a need for effective sanctions against non-payers to protect the interests of those that do pay and to generate income for the upkeep of the stock. There is also a need to protect tenants from the anti-social behaviour of others. Further, the interference is proportional since the right to possession is not automatic. Possession can only be obtained by following the statutory procedure. The fact that introductory tenancies are time limited also helps to make the interference proportionate.[201] However, all this means is that the legislation does not breach the Convention because it does not require the authority to act in a disproportionate manner. This does not rule out the possibility that they may act disproportionately in an individual case, for example if they acted on no evidence in which case they would be subject to judicial review.

---

[199] *Johns*, this may seem surprising because judicial review is limited to questions of law rather than fact. However, second tier appeals on points of law only have been found to be sufficient to put right any defective procedure. See *Stefan v UK* (1997) 25 EHRR CD 130 and *X v UK* (1998) 25 EHRR CD. In *Johns* the court thought that although judicial review was limited to points of law this does allow for a limited factual enquiry in that the decision could be quashed if the decision maker acted on no evidence, or came to an unreasonable conclusion from the evidence before them. See *Ashbridge v Minister of Housing and Local Government* [1965] 1 WLR 1320. Decisions can also be quashed if they take into account irrelevant considerations. However, the opposite view was taken in *R (on the application of Alconbury Developments and others) v Secretary of State for Environment, Transport and the Regions* (2000) CO/3742/2000, where *Johns* was distinguished. The critical difference in *Alconbury* was that the Secretary of State was responsible for planning policy and decision taking, whereas for introductory tenancies the council decides the reasons for seeking possession but it is the decision of the reviewing officer which is subject to judicial review and not of the higher policy maker. This seems a rather fine distinction, but appears to leave open the possibility to challenge a council policy as to the circumstances under which it will seek possession.

[200] See Section 4.4 above and *Mazari v Italy* 1999 28 EHRR CD 175 and *Buckley v UK* (1996) 23 EHRR 101.

[201] See *Johns* note 199.

4.5.3 There remains the issue of whether the use of introductory tenancies is discriminatory (Article 8 in conjunction with Article 14). Although this issue has not been strictly decided by the courts it seems unlikely that they are because, where the local authority adopts the scheme, all tenants will initially have introductory tenancies. There is a slight possibility that they may be considered discriminatory on the grounds of geographical location, since the scheme is not mandatory and can be adopted locally. However, such discrimination may well be within the margin of appreciation because there will probably be sound policy reasons for making the scheme an optional one. The decision of the council to adopt a scheme may be open to challenge but it would be very difficult to prove that the adoption is a disproportionate response since rent arrears and anti-social behaviour are virtually universal housing management problems.

4.6 **Housing benefit and housing benefit fraud.** *Article 6, Article 8.*

4.6.1 The caselaw of the ECHR points strongly to housing benefit being a "civil right" for the purposes of Article 6 (see paragraph 3.2.1 above). Accordingly, where there is a dispute as to entitlement, the claimant is entitled to a hearing before an impartial tribunal. Prior to 2 July 2001 disputes were dealt with by Housing Benefit Review Boards (HBRB), consisting entirely of councillors of the authority whose officers made the original decision. It was not, therefore, an impartial tribunal as required by Article 6, although in some circumstances the availability of judicial review may "cure" procedural irregularities (see paragraph 3.2.4 above)[202]. As from 2 July 2001 responsibility for the adjudication of appeals has been transferred to the Appeals Service (formerly Social Security Appeals Tribunal). This will deal with the Article 6 point (on the assumption that the tribunal does satisfy the Article 6 criteria) from July 2001, but does not deal with HBRB decisions made between 2 October 2000 to 1 July 2001. Despite the new arrangements there may be scope for challenging decisions to restrict the rent. Although there is a system of internal reviews by the Rent Service (Rent Officer Service in Wales) the decision maker (including the Appeals Service) must accept the Rent Service assessment as fact. It remains to be seen whether judicial review will be judged to be a sufficient back-stop.[203]

---

[202] See also *Bryan v UK* (1995) 21 EHRR 342, a planning law matter where the ECHR held that an appeal to the Inspector against an enforcement notice was not to an independent and impartial tribunal but that subsequent appeal to the High Court cured the defect even though the powers of the Court were limited by statute. See also *Johns* and *Alconbury* notes 116 and 199.

[203] For a detailed discussion on these potential Article 6 challenges see *Journal of Housing Law*, Volume 4, Issue 4, July/August 2001.

4.6.2 On 2 July 2001 the discretionary additional benefit payments for exceptional circumstances were abolished and replaced by Discretionary Housing Payments.[204] These serve the same purpose as exceptional hardship payments and like their predecessor are subject to cash limits. However, unlike exceptional hardship payments they are not part of the benefits system and so are not subject to the new appeal arrangements. The Government's objective in detaching the assistance from housing benefit is to produce a purely discretionary scheme which is outside the social security system and not subject to the new right of appeal to an Appeal Tribunal. The process for challenging decisions will be an internal review and thereafter judicial review. The Government's view is that by breaking the link with the benefits system and making payments wholly discretionary their payment cannot constitute a civil right thus avoiding the possibility of an Article 6 challenge. It remains to be seen if this reasoning is robust.

Other substantive areas of Housing Benefit may need to be revisited in light of the Act, for example the rules surrounding single parents (mainly fathers) who have regular weekly contact with their children, but which is not taken account of in entitlement. There may be scope for similar challenges to the substantive rules particularly when tied to an Article 14 challenge (prohibition on discrimination), but generally these are beyond the scope of this work.[205]

4.6.3 Procedures to be followed in criminal investigations is generally beyond the scope of this Guide and so only an outline is provided. [206] Challenges may be expected on the procedures used to collect evidence to prosecute claimants accused of housing benefit fraud. One area which may be subject to particular scrutiny is the use of surveillance and covert intelligence to collect evidence (Article 8). All surveillance must be in accordance with the law which is now set out in the Regulation of Investigatory Powers Act 2000 (RIP Act). A basic principle of the RIP Act is that all investigation has to be accounted for. Normally this will require the extent of the investigation to be determined and authorised by a senior officer. Guidance for fraud officers has been issued by the Department for Work and Pensions (formerly the Department of Social Security) and the Home Office.[207]

---

[204] Child Support, Pensions and Social Security Act 2000, Section 69 and The Discretionary Financial Assistance Regulations 2001 SI 2001 No. 1167.

[205] For an introduction to the Human Rights Act implications for social security generally see *Legal Action*, September 2000.

[206] For a useful introduction to this subject see *Legal Action*, November 2000, 'The Human Rights Act: points for defence lawyers'.

[207] HB Circulars HB/CTB F6 & F9/2000, see also Home Office website www.homeoffice.gov.uk. ripa.ripact.htm

4.6.4 Further areas which are likely to be the subjects of challenge include the use of inspectors' powers and the imposition of administrative penalties as an alternative to prosecution. [208] In particular the use of penalties may be challenged under Article 6(2) if they are used as an alternative to prosecution where it is doubtful whether the evidence would be sufficient to secure a conviction. Landlords, including RSLs may also challenge the use of inspectors' powers which are very widely drawn, if they are exercised in a heavy-handed or arbitrary way. [209]

4.7 **Right to buy.** *First Protocol, Article 1.*

4.7.1 Secure tenants (and assured tenants who were formerly secure tenants prior to stock transfer) have the right to buy. This may be a "possession" for the purposes of Article 1. Accordingly, if the right to buy were removed, that would amount to a deprivation of a possession. However, if any new legislation removing the right applied only to new tenants they would not be able to claim a breach of the Convention: they have not been deprived of a possession since they would have never benefited from it in the first place.

4.8 **Responsibility of housing provider to tackle anti-social behaviour.** *Article 8.*

4.8.1 There is no implied term in a lease or tenancy agreement which makes a landlord liable to a tenant for failure to deal with anti-social behaviour by another of its tenants.[210] The landlord has the power, but not the duty, to take action against the offending tenant (although a failure to take adequate action may lead to a successful complaint of maladministration to the Ombudsman). However, where the tenancy agreement does impose such an obligation or where it can be shown that the tenant has suffered loss caused by another person due to the negligence of the landlord a right of action by that tenant against the landlord may exist.[211]

4.8.2 The Convention is designed to protect the individual citizen and private organisations against infringement of fundamental rights by the state and state organisations. Thus, in most cases of criminal or anti-social behaviour by a private individual they are not covered by the Convention. As a general rule, where the interference is coming from

---

[208] Administrative penalties, see Social Security Administration Act 1992, Section 115A.
[209] Inspectors have wide powers to enter business premises (including landlords) and the right to examine documents relating to anyone believed to be a benefit claimant. Social Security Administration Act 1992, Section 110A.
[210] See *Hussain v Lancaster City Council*, [2000] 1 QB 1.
[211] But early indications are that the courts will be reluctant to impose this burden on local authorities, see *Mowan* notes 69 and 214.

some body other than a public one, the Convention is not applicable.[212] In general, therefore, anti-social and criminal behaviour by an individual which causes nuisance to neighbours is not covered by the Convention.

4.8.3 However, in some cases, the ECHR has been prepared to extend the limits of the Convention so as to impose positive duties on member states to take action in order to ensure that Convention rights of one person are not violated by another: (see further Sections 1.2 and 2.3 above). Article 8 is designed to protect the peaceful enjoyment of an individual's home and privacy, and Article 3 is designed to protect against inhuman and degrading treatment, so the state is expected to take reasonable steps to protect those interests.[213] Whether the state has an obligation to intervene will depend on the extent and type of the abuse and the steps that have actually been taken. Article 8[214] may be violated by anti-social behaviour by another tenant. If a public authority fails to use the powers[215] that it has to deal with the anti-social behaviour by another tenant, it may be in violation of the Act unless it can show that it has carefully and responsibly weighed all the facts and taken a reasonable decision which is within the "margin of appreciation".[216]

4.9 Use of powers against individuals accused of anti-social behaviour
Article 6, Article 8 and Article 14.

4.9.1 The use of powers to control anti-social behaviour has been the subject to a number of challenges since the Act came into force in October 2000. Fears that the Act would be used as a "charter for criminals" who routinely raise Human Rights Act defences have proved unfounded. Perhaps, unsurprisingly, the courts have taken a more cautious approach and have given the state the benefit of a wide margin of appreciation. As at July 2001, no declarations of incompatibility have been made in respect of the various pieces of recent social legislation designed to tackle anti-social behaviour.

---

[212] See *Mowan v Wandsworth & Another* (2001) 33 HLR 56.
[213] See *Whiteside v UK* (1994) 76 – A DR 80. The applicant complained that the state did not do sufficient to protect her from the violent actions of her former partner – although she did not succeed the court recognised that the scale of her difficulties put the state under a positive obligation to protect against this type of abuse.
[214] See, for example, *Arondelle v UK (1982)* 26 DR 5 (noise from Gatwick airport) and *Powell and Rayner v UK* (1990) 12 EHRR 355. However, in *Mowan*, the Human Rights Act implications were raised, the court approved of *Hussian* see note 210 above. The rule in Hussain was so well established that the common law could not be construed in a way that would effectively create a new cause of action by aggrieved tenants against their landlord. To do so would extend the role of the court beyond its constitutional function of interpreter and adjudicator to one of legislator.
[215] As to the range of powers open to housing providers, see generally Hunter and Bretherton (1998) *Anti-social Behaviour: Law and Practice in the Management of Social Housing*, Lemos and Crane.
[216] But see *Mowan*, notes 69 and 214 above.

4.9.2 In general terms challenges can be expected or have already been made in respect of the **procedure** used to apply some power of restraint (Article 6) and the **effect** of any power once it has been granted (Article 8). Aspects of the law which either have already been or are likely to be challenged include:

- introductory tenancies [217](see Section 4.5);
- anti-social behaviour orders;[218]
- protection from harassment;[219]
- public order and criminal trespass;[220]
- possession proceedings (see Section 4.4);
- the use of injunctions;
- the use of CCTV and the covert collection of evidence (see paragraph 4.6.3)

4.9.3 The procedures for obtaining anti-social behaviour orders have already survived challenges of their compatibility with the Convention. In *McCann*,[221] the subject of an anti-social behaviour order argued that the proceedings to obtain an order were criminal and therefore as the subject of the proceedings they were entitled to the minimum rights accorded to the accused in criminal trials by Article 6(2) and (3), whereas the burden of proof required to obtain an order was only of the lower civil standard. Applying ECHR jurisprudence to the question of whether the proceedings were civil or criminal, the Court of Appeal held that regard should be had as to: how the proceedings were categorised in domestic law; the nature of the offence and the severity of the penalty imposed. The court found that the proceedings were not criminal because, amongst other things, no penalty was imposed.[222] In a separate Article 6 challenge the civil proceedings have been challenged as unfair, on the grounds that the subject of the order would only be able to properly challenge the evidence through cross examination if the witnesses were identified.

---

217 Housing Act 1996, Part V, Chapter I.
218 Crime and Disorder Act 1998, Section 1.
219 Protection from Harassment Act 1997.
220 Criminal Justice and Public Order Act, Part V.
221 *R (on the application of McCann) v Manchester Crown Court* [2001] EWCA Civ 281.
222 See *McCann*. The imposition of an anti-social behaviour order (ASBO) was not itself a penalty, a penalty was only imposed if the order was breached, in this sense an ASBO was similar to an injunction. The clear purpose of ASBOs was, like an injunction, to prevent future harm, rather than punish for past behaviour (see Crime and Disorder Act 1998, Section 1(1)(b)). Further in seeking an order, unlike public order offences, it was not necessary to prove that the subject of it had either used threatening behaviour or acted with criminal intent, rather it was only necessary to prove that their behaviour was such that it was likely to cause distress. It was also the clear intention of Parliament that the proceedings should be civil, precisely because there was a lower standard of proof, thus making it easier to prevent future harm.

Further, despite the fact that an order is likely to impose serious restrictions on the subject, the procedure allowed for the admission of hearsay evidence. Both of these arguments were rejected, there was no presumption in human rights law that hearsay evidence should be excluded in civil trials, therefore it followed that there could be no presumption that there was a right to cross-examine witnesses. The trial would be fair because in assessing the evidence before it the court would give proper consideration as to the weight to be applied to the evidence and in doing so the court was obliged to act in a way that was compatible with the Convention.[223]

Despite the procedure being sound, human rights considerations come into play when the *powers* conferred by the Crime and Disorder Act are *exercised* because there is a risk that a number of the Articles could be infringed (for example Article 8 and Article 11). In order to avoid this risk "the principle of proportionality must be carefully observed".[224] For the position on possession proceedings see Section 4.4 (eviction) and 4.5 (introductory tenancies) above. An outright possession order for anti-social behaviour is not necessarily disproportionate, particularly if the facts are not in dispute and nothing less will achieve the purpose of protecting the victim. [225]

4.10   Environmental pollution. *Article 8.*

4.10.1 Where tenants are suffering from the effects of environmental pollution which the public authority has failed to deal with effectively, there may be a Convention violation. In *Lopez Ostra v Spain*[226] pollution was being produced by local industry, partially funded by the local authority, on land provided by the local authority. The industry caused severe pollution and nuisance to those in nearby houses. The authority rehoused some of those affected and took some action to stop some of the pollution. The ECHR decided that there was a violation of the applicants' right to respect for "home and family life" through the failure of the authority to take effective action. The court decided that the authority had to have regard to the fair balance that has to be struck between the competing interests of the individual and the community as a whole. In striking that balance, economics and the rights and freedoms of others are relevant. In this case, the balance had not been achieved.

---

[223] *R v Marylebone Magistrates Court ex parte Clingham* [2001] EWCA ADMIN 1, compare with *Bates* note 192 above.

[224] See *McCann* above.

[225] *London Borough of Lambeth v Howard* [2001] EWCA Civ 468. Here the tenant had already been convicted of an offence under the Protection from Harassment Act 1997 and there was an injunction banning him from returning to the property.

[226] (1994) 20 EHRR 277.

4.10.2 A similar result was achieved in another case.[227] By contrast, in the two airport cases involving the UK,[228] although the ECHR held that the aircraft noise pollution did amount to a violation of the Article 8(1) rights, the failure of the public authority to take effective action was justifiable.

4.10.3 The relevance of these cases for local authorities and RSLs is as follows. Where there is nuisance or pollution which affects the Convention rights of their tenants, the housing provider may be liable (even if it was not directly responsible for producing the nuisance or pollution) if it fails to do something that is within its powers so as to prevent the violation of the Convention rights.

4.11 **Repairs and maintenance.** *Articles 3, 6 and 8 and First Protocol, Article 1.*

4.11.1 As already stated, the Convention does not guarantee a right to housing. Nor does it have anything to say, directly, about the quality of any housing that is provided by anyone. Landlord and tenant law does provide some protection by placing an obligation on the landlord to keep in repair the structure, exterior and installations in the dwelling.[229] However, obligations on landlords are generally limited to "repairs" and not to remedy unsatisfactory or degrading housing conditions such as dampness or mould growth caused by structural defects or design.[230] Where the landlord lets unfurnished accommodation there is generally no obligation to ensure that it is fit for habitation.[231] Although generally only the tenant can enforce a covenant to repair in a tenancy agreement, other members of a tenant's family (and sometimes their visitors) may have rights under other legislation: for example, Section 4 of the Defective Premises Act 1972 provides that where a landlord is under an obligation to maintain or repair the premises (including a right to enter to do works which are not specifically the tenant's obligations) the landlord is under a duty towards *'all persons who might reasonably be expected to be affected by defects in the state of the premises'*.[232]

---

[227] *Guerra v Italy* (1998) 26 EHRR 357.

[228] See note 214 above.

[229] See Landlord and Tenant Act 1985, Sections 11-17. The landlord also has an implied obligation to repair the means of access to the accommodation in certain circumstances e.g. lifts and lighting in a high rise block of flats – *Liverpool City Council v Irwin* [1977] AC 239.

[230] *Quick v Taff Ely BC* [1986] QB 809.

[231] *Smith v Marrable* (1843) 11 M&W 5, *Cavalier v Pope* [1906] AC 428, *Southwark v Mills* (2000) 32 HLR 148. Although there are still a very small number of cases where there is an obligation if the tenancy is let at a "low rent", Landlord and Tenant Act 1985, Section 8.

[232] Other occupiers may benefit from a landlord's duty of care towards the tenant's invitees in the parts of the premises which remain the responsibility of the landlord (e.g. common parts in flats including stairs and lifts etc.) See Occupiers Liability Act 1957.

So far as the home is in disrepair, the tenant potentially has a range of remedies [233] to enforce their landlord obligations which are "civil rights" for the purposes of Article 6. Housing lawyers have criticised these remedies as being "slow, costly and ineffective"[234] but they do represent the only way tenants can be adequately compensated in damages for failure to repair and the procedural difficulties associated with the type of action are by no means as severe as in Scotland.[235] The alternative route of using Section 82 of the Environmental Protection Act 1990 (statutory nuisance) is the path now favoured by most specialist housing lawyers in England. However, although this will lead to an order for works to be carried out only nominal amounts of compensation can be ordered. The absence of an effective remedy to pursue an Article 8 right may amount to a violation of Article 6: the right of access to a fair hearing to determine a civil right.[236] Further, Article 1 of the First Protocol may come into play since a repairing covenant is a "possession".[237] So, for example, there may be a breach of this Article if a public authority has a repairs schedule which gives a low priority to a particular type of repair. The lack of access to legal aid where a claim is confined to the small claims court, or to pursue a private prosecution for a breach of a statutory nuisance may infringe the tenant's Article 6 right of access to a fair hearing. However, in the case of statutory nuisance claims this may be remedied by the conditional fee arrangements. In addition the Civil Procedure Rules reduce the small claims threshold for housing disrepair cases.[238]

---

[233] Remedies include: for contractual obligations, an order for specific performance, a declaration of the tenants' rights allowing them to carry out the repairs themselves (Section 38 County Court Act 1938 and Civil Procedure Rules rule 25.1) and damages which take into account inconvenience and diminution in value of the tenancy. For non-contractual obligations a mandatory injunction and damages.

[234] Luba (1991) *Repairs: Tenants Rights*, Second Edition, at page 65, Legal Action Group.

[235] See note 236 below.

[236] Although the situation in England and Wales is far from perfect it is by no means as difficult as in Scotland where applications for statutory nuisance have floundered on a sea of technical difficulty. Further in Scotland there have been no reported cases of a successful application for specific implement involving disrepair. Article 13 of the Convention guarantees the right to an effective remedy for a violation of a Convention right. Article 13 is not included in the 1998 Act. The reason for this is that the Government is of the view that the very fact of the 1998 Act itself provides an effective remedy. Some would disagree with this assertion. Nevertheless, the statements made by Lord Irvine to this effect in the House of Lords may be relied upon in any argument to the effect that there is a violation of a Convention right as a result of the ineffectiveness of any remedy. However, in England and Wales although actions for breach of repairing covenant are by no means straightforward, successful applications for specific performance are not unheard of and successful actions for statutory nuisance are fairly common. It is therefore unlikely that courts in England would conclude that there is a failure to provide an effective remedy.

[237] *S v UK* (1986) 1 DR 226.

[238] Civil Procedure Rules 1998 r27.1(2).

4.11.2 It is easy to see how severe disrepair or statutory nuisance ma[...] a failure to "respect for the home" and that the effects of disrepa[...] (especially dampness) may interfere with "family and private life" [...] may amount to a violation of Article 8 or in extreme cases Article 3. [...] are a number of ways in which the common law could develop and the[...] include:

- whether tenants of unfurnished accommodation will benefit from a new implied term of fit for habitation;
- whether structural defects which lead to unfitness will continue to be excluded from the definition of repair;
- whether obligations to action unfitness will require a public authority to proactively tackle their own unfit stock.

These are, of course, not just minor technical legal issues about legal rights. Any change which expanded repairs to include improvements could have a huge impact on the repairs budgets of local authority landlords, a factor which may influence the courts in any future decision.[239]

4.12 Rent levels and rent control. *Article 8, First Protocol, Article 1.*

4.12.1 Given that the purpose of the Convention is not to guarantee social or economic rights, in particular there is no duty on a public authority to provide housing, it seems unlikely that anything in the Convention restricts the level of rents charged by public landlords. Even if this were not the case, the availability of housing benefit (albeit at somewhat lower levels than at one time) to those on low incomes and the fair rent regime still applicable to some tenancies would suggest that the Act cannot be used to argue for a particular content to "affordable rents" in the RSL sector nor lower rents in the other housing sectors. Such cases as have been decided by the ECHR have been taken by private landlords alleging a breach of the First Protocol, Article 1 due to rent controls. They lost.[240]

4.13 Succession and transfer of tenancies. *Article 8.*

4.13.1 Those entitled to succeed to a secure tenancy on the death of a secure tenant include the resident spouse, someone living with the tenant as

---

[239] See, for example, *Oakley v Birmingham City Council* (2001) 33 HLR 30, a statutory nuisance prosecution. Although human rights issues were not raised in *Oakley*, it does nevertheless demonstrate how the courts are reluctant to expand the law where there are likely to be significant social, political or economic consequences, this properly is a role for Parliament. Such considerations are likely to come into play when determining whether the state is within the "margin of appreciation".

[240] *Mellacher v Austria* (1989) 12 EHRR 391. ECHR decisions on rent controls and security of tenure can be found at notes 158 and 166-168 of this Guide.

' and members of the family resident in the house for
ᵉ date of death.[241] Those entitled to succeed to an
the spouse or someone living with the tenant as
The position of (Rent Act) regulated tenants is more
ᵉ death of the original tenant (whether they were a
ry tenant) the surviving spouse is entitled to
...ᵤᵗ.ᵤₜory tenancy. A person who was living with the original
tenant at the time of their death as "his or her wife or husband" is treated
as their spouse and so would also be entitled to a statutory tenancy. If no
one is entitled to succeed as a spouse then a person who had been living
with the original tenant for a period of two years as a "member of their
family" immediately prior to their death would be entitled to succeed to
an assured tenancy. What then is the position with regard to same sex
couples?

4.13.2 In *Fitzpatrick v Sterling Housing Association*, the plaintiff was the resident
same-sex partner of a (Rent Act) statutory tenant who died.[242] It was held
that although he could not succeed to a statutory tenancy, they were
entitled to succeed to an assured tenancy as a "member of the family".
However, in reaching this conclusion the House of Lords made it clear
that they could do so for Rent Act tenancies only because the phrase
"member of the family" was not prescribed by the legislation. They
indicated that the same position would not necessarily follow for secure
tenancies where the legislation was more prescriptive.[243] They also
approved their earlier decision that in order for the survivor to be treated
as a surviving spouse, and so succeed to a statutory tenancy, the phrase
"his or her wife or husband", could only mean a partner of the opposite
sex.[244] Whether the legislation is discriminatory against same-sex couples
for secure, regulated or assured tenancies remains to be seen.[245] The
ECHR has in the past taken an unsympathetic view. In *S v UK*,[246] the
applicant was the lesbian partner of the deceased secure tenant who was
refused succession rights. She claimed a failure to respect for her home.

---

[241] Housing Act 1985, Section 87.

[242] *Fitzpatrick v Sterling Housing Association* [1999] 3 WLR 1113, note that Sterling Housing
Association was not a Registered Social Landlord so the tenant was not a secure tenant but a
Rent Act regulated tenant.

[243] See Housing Act 1985, Section 113.

[244] See *Harrogate BC v Simpson* (1984) 17 HLR 205, a decision relating to secure tenancies. This
decision was subsequently challenged unsuccessfully at the ECHR in *S v UK* (1986) 47 DR 274.

[245] The question is whether it is discriminatory against non-married couples not whether it is
allowable to discriminate in favour of married couples. Marriage is a formal legal relationship
with rights and responsibilities so it is not generally discriminatory to favour married over
non-married couples.

[246] (1986) 47 DR 274, the same applicant as in *Simpson*, see note 244 above.

The Commission held that the application was inadmissible, as she had no contractual right to the property. On the death of her partner, she had no right to stay in the house so that it could not be regarded as a "home" for the purposes of the Convention. The Commission declared that any discrimination was justified on the grounds that heterosexual family life deserves greater protection than homosexual life.

4.13.3 The Convention is a living instrument, however, and the ECHR and the Commission have shown a growing acceptance of the rights of homosexuals and gay couples.[247] That has resulted in the recent case of *Salgueiro da Silva Mouta v Portugal*,[248] where the court held that the refusal of a Portuguese court to allow a gay father residence rights regarding his child, on the grounds of his homosexuality, was not only a breach of Article 8 but was unlawfully discriminatory under Article 14. Thus, it could now be argued that under ECHR caselaw a same-sex couple must be treated the same way as an unmarried mixed-sex couple.[249] In Scotland, the Housing (Scotland) Act 2001 now provides that succession to the Scottish Secure Tenancy is available to same-sex partners.[250]

4.14 **Compulsory purchase, demolition and slum clearance.** *Article 6, First Protocol, Article 1.*

4.14.1 Compulsory purchase is deprivation of property, but since the power to compulsory purchase only exists where authorised by statute it will be "in accordance with the law". Therefore, the question to be decided is whether the acquisition is in the public interest and according to the general principles of international law (for example, the right to be compensated). The use and procedures for exercising Housing Act powers is an area where challenges can be expected. For example, the service of notices and independent rights to appeal.[251] The prospects for success will depend upon the particular legislation under which the powers are being exercised.

---

[247] e.g. *Sutherland v UK* [1996] EHLRR 554 (violation of Article 8 and 14 in the differential age of consent for gay and heterosexual couples), a case departing from the Commission's previous caselaw in this area.

[248] App. No. 33290/96, decided by the ECHR on 21 December 1999.

[249] The position in European Community law is different: see case T-264/97 *D v Council* (28 January 1998) unreported and *Grant v South West Trains* [1998] All ER (EC) 193, ECJ (13 judge court) (lesbian denied travel pass for her lover; the comparator was that of a gay man, not a heterosexual couple). It is thought that the *Silva Mouta* case now undermines the authority of that decision. Note that in the case of secure or assured tenancies the court could only grant a declaration because *Fitzpatrick* upheld the position in *Simpson*.

[250] Sections 22 and 108.

[251] See Housing Act 1985, part IX.

4.15 **Housing management records and the collection of personal data.** *Article 8.*

4.15.1 This is an area where the Convention has already had a huge influence on UK law, ultimately resulting in a number of UK statutes regulating the position how data is acquired, recorded and used.[252] However, UK data protection legislation covers a far wider constituency than the Convention which only seeks to regulate the role of the state against individuals, whereas the Data Protection Act regulates any organisation who holds personal data, not just the state.

4.15.2 The legitimate collection of personal data and its use is likely to have a significant impact on housing management practice in several areas. A by no means exhaustive list of areas likely to be affected includes:

- data sharing and joint working, for example community care;
- tackling crime and anti-social behaviour;
- community safety (e.g. the housing of sex offenders and use of CCTV);
- rent recording and access to records (e.g. credit references);
- use of data for strategic initiatives (e.g. anti-poverty strategies);
- housing benefit fraud.

The use, collection of and access to, personal data is a huge subject and well beyond the scope of this Guide, not least because of the wider and more extensive coverage afforded by the data protection legislation. For further guidance on this subject see the Chartered Institute of Housing in Scotland Guide by the same author. [253]

---

[252] The Data Protection Act 1984 was passed because the UK provided virtually no protection for subjects whose data was held on computers and so could not guarantee Article 8 rights. The Act was passed in response to the potential threat that the UK would be cut off from direct computer links with Europe. The Interception of Communications Act 1985 and the Access to Personal Files Act 1987 regulating the collection of and access to personal data were both passed as a result of successful challenges against the UK in the ECHR. See *Malone*, case 8691/79 (telephone tapping) and *Gaskin* case 10454/83 (access to personal records held by a local authority). The Data Protection Act 1984 and the Access to Personal Files Act 1987 have since been superseded by the Data Protection Act 1998.

[253] See Section 6 of this Guide, 'Further Sources and References', see also the Office of the Information Commissioner (formerly known as the Data Protection Commissioner), www.dataprotection.gov.uk

5: ENFORCEMENT OF THE ACT

5.1 It is beyond the scope of this Guide to give any detailed guidance of the enforcement mechanisms in the Act. The way in which the Act is enforced is summarised below. Much further detail can be obtained from the sources listed in Section 6 of this Guide.

5.2 Although the Act came into force on 2 October 2000, any acts or omissions of public authorities prior to that date may be relied on in legal proceedings initiated by the public authority after that date. There is a limitation period of one year,[254] starting with the date on which the act complained of took place. That period may be extended if this would be "equitable".[255] No such limitation applies where a Convention right is raised as a defence by a victim to proceedings brought by a public authority.[256]

5.3 If a public authority has acted in breach of a Convention right, proceedings may be taken against it seeking damages. The court and procedure will be specified in Rules of Court.[257] Damages may only be awarded if the court has the power in general to award damages.[258] So, for example, an Appeals Tribunal may not award damages. No award of damages may be made unless the court is satisfied that it is necessary in order to give "just satisfaction". The court must apply the principles of the ECHR in assessing damages rather than the usual principles.[259]

5.4 The court, under Section 8 of the Act, may also make any other order, which is within its powers, as it considers just and appropriate. This could include an injunction (an order forbidding a certain act), an order for specific performance (an order to do something) or a declaration (a statement of the parties' legal rights). Interim remedies are also available:

---

[254] Section 7(1)(a) of the Act.
[255] Section 7(5)(b). Note that this one year period is subject to any other time limit of a shorter period. For example, three months is the time limit for an application to the Employment Tribunal. As for judicial review the normal time limit is three months, although any unreasonable delay, may be fatal to the case.
[256] Section 7.
[257] Section 7.
[258] Section 8.
[259] See Reid (1998), pages 397 to 426 for summaries of awards by the ECHR.

such as interim injunction in the case of threatened action which may breach the Convention rights of the applicant. However, certain restrictions are placed on interim remedies in the case of freedom of expression cases.[260] The person who takes the legal proceedings must be a "victim" for the purposes of the Convention (see Section 2.4 above).

5.5   If the act or omission complained of is that of a court or tribunal, the Convention claim can only be raised by way of appeal.[261]

5.6   A claim that a Convention right has been violated can also be raised as a defence in any court or tribunal proceedings. A counterclaim may also be lodged seeking a remedy.

5.7   If a court finds that primary legislation (such as an Act of the Westminster Parliament) violates the Convention, it does not have the power to strike it down. All it may do is to make a "declaration of incompatibility".[262] Government ministers are given special powers then to take "remedial action".[263] This may involve using a special procedure to amend the offending legislation.

---

[260] Section 12.
[261] Section 9.
[262] Section 4.
[263] Section 10 and Sch. 2.

6: FURTHER SOURCES AND REFERENCES

There has been a vast amount of literature published on this subject in the last few years in the UK. Much more has been published in the UK and abroad since the Convention was agreed in 1950. It is impossible to list all of the possible sources. Below are listed a number of texts which have been recently published. Many of them have been consulted in the course of the preparation of this Guide. Also included below are a number of useful websites.

Cases

There are a number of series of cases. There is the official series and also those produced by private publishers. By far the most useful and most accessible for the non-specialist is the European Human Rights Reports (referred to in the footnotes above as EHRR), published by Sweet and Maxwell and edited by T. Elicke and N. Grief. There are also a number of digests or summaries available of selected cases. They include:

V. Berger (1989), *Caselaw of the ECHR* (3 volumes), The Round Press (Dublin)

S. Farran (1996), *The United Kingdom before the ECHR: Case Law and Commentaries*, Blackstone Press Ltd

S. Nash and M. Furse (eds.) (1999), *Essential Human Rights Cases*, Jordans

K. Starmer, I. Byrne and F. Klug (2001), *Human Rights Digest*, Blackstones (on CD Rom and in book form.)

Reference Books

C. Baker (1998), *Human Rights Act 1998: A Practitioner's Guide*, Sweet and Maxwell

L. Betten (ed.) (1999), *The Human Rights Act 1998: What it Means*, Martinus Nijhoff Publishers

L. Clements, N. Mole and A. Simmons (1998), *European Human Rights: Taking a Case under the Convention*, Sweet and Maxwell

Lord Clyde and D. Edwards (2000), *Judicial Review*, W. Green

J. Coppel (1999), *The Human Rights Act 1998*, Wiley

P. Duffy, S. Grosz and J. Beatson (1999), *A Guide to the Human Rights Act 1998*, Sweet and Maxwell

B. Emmerson and J. Simor (2000), *Human Rights Practice* (looseleaf), Sweet and Maxwell

D. J. Harris, M. O'Boyle and C. Warbrick (1995), *Law of the European Convention on Human Rights*, Butterworths

M. Hunt (1997), *Using Human Rights Law in the English Courts*, Hart Publishing

A. Lester and D. Oliver (1997), *Constitutional Law and Human Rights*, Butterworths

A. Lester and D. Pannick (eds.) (1999), *Human Rights Law and Practice*, Butterworths

D. O'Carroll (2000), *The Data Protection Act 1998: A Guide for Housing Professionals*, Chartered Institute of Housing in Scotland

K. Reid (1998), *A Practitioner's Guide to the European Convention of Human Rights*, Sweet and Maxwell

K. Starmer (1999), *European Human Rights Law*, Legal Action Group

M. Supperstone, J. Goudie and J. Coppel (1999), *Local Authorities and the Human Rights Act 1998*, Butterworths

K. Tonge, T. Grundy and A. Stark (forthcoming, 2002) *Human Rights for Housing Officers: A Guide to Proofing Day-to-day Practice*, Chartered Institute of Housing/ Joseph Rowntree Foundation

J. Wadham and H. Mountfield (1999), *Blackstone's Guide to the Human Rights Act 1998*, Blackstone Press Ltd

Websites

http://www.hmso.gov.uk/acts.htm
All Acts of the Westminster Parliament from 1997 including the Human Rights Act 1998.

http://www.casetrack.com
Subscriber website where full text of latest High Court judgments can be downloaded. Site run by Smith Bernal, Official Shorthand Writers to the Court.

http://www.echr.coe.int/
The Council of Europe's website. Lots of information on the Convention and a searchable database of ECHR and Commission decisions.

http://www.beagle.org.uk/hra
A good free website with a lot of human rights materials.

http//www.liberty-human-rights.org.uk/
Website of Liberty a UK-based human rights organisation.

http://www.yale.edu/lawweb/avalon/diana/index.html
A huge database of links to human rights websites.

http://www.wcl.american.edu/pub/humright/brief
An online human rights journal.

http://www.lib.uchicago.edu/e/law/intl.html#human
Another huge database of links to human rights websites.

APPENDIX 1: EUROPEAN CONVENTION ON HUMAN RIGHTS: AN ABRIDGED TEXT

The following is the text of most of the Articles of the Convention which are incorporated into the 1998 Act. *Not all are incorporated, notably Article 13 (see note 236 of this Guide).* The full version of the Act may be found on the HMSO website (address given above) or in most of the texts listed above which contain the name of the Act in the title. The full text of the Convention can be found in the Council of Europe website (address given above) or in Reid (1998), above, among other sources.

Articles of the Convention incorporated in the 1998 Act

Rights and freedoms

ARTICLE 2
RIGHT TO LIFE
1. Everyone's right to life shall be protected by law. No one shall be deprived of his life intentionally save in the execution of a sentence of a court following his conviction of a crime for which this penalty is provided by law.
2. Deprivation of life shall not be regarded as inflicted in contravention of this Article when it results from the use of force which is no more than absolutely necessary:
   (a) in defence of any person from unlawful violence;
   (b) in order to effect a lawful arrest or to prevent the escape of a person lawfully detained;
   (c) in action lawfully taken for the purpose of quelling a riot or insurrection.

ARTICLE 3
PROHIBITION OF TORTURE
No one shall be subjected to torture or to inhuman or degrading treatment or punishment.

ARTICLE 4
PROHIBITION OF SLAVERY AND FORCED LABOUR
1. No one shall be held in slavery or servitude.
2. No one shall be required to perform forced or compulsory labour.

3. For the purpose of this Article the term "forced or compulsory labour" shall not include:
    (a) any work required to be done in the ordinary course of detention imposed according to the provisions of Article 5 of this Convention or during conditional release from such detention;
    (b) any service of a military character or, in case of conscientious objectors in countries where they are recognised, service exacted instead of compulsory military service;
    (c) any service exacted in case of an emergency or calamity threatening the life or well-being of the community;
    (d) any work or service which forms part of normal civic obligations.

ARTICLE 5
RIGHT TO LIBERTY AND SECURITY

1. Everyone has the right to liberty and security of person. No one shall be deprived of his liberty save in the following cases and in accordance with a procedure prescribed by law:
    (a) the lawful detention of a person after conviction by a competent court;
    (b) the lawful arrest or detention of a person for non-compliance with the lawful order of a court or in order to secure the fulfilment of any obligation prescribed by law;
    (c) the lawful arrest or detention of a person effected for the purpose of bringing him before the competent legal authority on reasonable suspicion of having committed an offence or when it is reasonably considered necessary to prevent his committing an offence or fleeing after having done so;
    (d) the detention of a minor by lawful order for the purpose of educational supervision or his lawful detention for the purpose of bringing him before the competent legal authority;
    (e) the lawful detention of persons for the prevention of the spreading of infectious diseases, of persons of unsound mind, alcoholics or drug addicts or vagrants;
    (f) the lawful arrest or detention of a person to prevent his effecting an unauthorised entry into the country or of a person against whom action is being taken with a view to deportation or extradition.
2. Everyone who is arrested shall be informed promptly, in a language which he understands, of the reasons for his arrest and of any charge against him.
3. Everyone arrested or detained in accordance with the provisions of paragraph 1(c) of this Article shall be brought promptly before a judge or other officer authorised by law to exercise judicial power and shall be entitled to trial within a reasonable time or to release pending trial. Release may be conditioned by guarantees to appear for trial.

4. Everyone who is deprived of his liberty by arrest or detention shall be entitled to take proceedings by which the lawfulness of his detention shall be decided speedily by a court and his release ordered if the detention is not lawful.
5. Everyone who has been the victim of arrest or detention in contravention of the provisions of this Article shall have an enforceable right to compensation.

ARTICLE 6
RIGHT TO A FAIR TRIAL

1. In the determination of his civil rights and obligations or of any criminal charge against him, everyone is entitled to a fair and public hearing within a reasonable time by an independent and impartial tribunal established by law. Judgment shall be pronounced publicly but the press and public may be excluded from all or part of the trial in the interest of morals, public order or national security in a democratic society, where the interests of juveniles or the protection of the private life of the parties so require, or to the extent strictly necessary in the opinion of the court in special circumstances where publicity would prejudice the interests of justice.
2. Everyone charged with a criminal offence shall be presumed innocent until proved guilty according to law.
3. Everyone charged with a criminal offence has the following minimum rights:
    (a) to be informed promptly, in a language which he understands and in detail, of the nature and cause of the accusation against him;
    (b) to have adequate time and facilities for the preparation of his defence;
    (c) to defend himself in person or through legal assistance of his own choosing or, if he has not sufficient means to pay for legal assistance, to be given it free when the interests of justice so require;
    (d) to examine or have examined witnesses against him and to obtain the attendance and examination of witnesses on his behalf under the same conditions as witnesses against him;
    (e) to have the free assistance of an interpreter if he cannot understand or speak the language used in court.

ARTICLE 7
NO PUNISHMENT WITHOUT LAW

1. No one shall be held guilty of any criminal offence on account of any act or omission which did not constitute a criminal offence under national or international law at the time when it was committed. Nor shall a heavier penalty be imposed than the one that was applicable at the time the criminal offence was committed.
2. This Article shall not prejudice the trial and punishment of any person for any act or omission which, at the time when it was committed, was criminal according to the general principles of law recognised by civilised nations.

ARTICLE 8
RIGHT TO RESPECT FOR PRIVATE AND FAMILY LIFE

1. Everyone has the right to respect for his private and family life, his home and his correspondence.
2. There shall be no interference by a public authority with the exercise of this right except such as is in accordance with the law and is necessary in a democratic society in the interests of national security, public safety or the economic well-being of the country, for the prevention of disorder or crime, for the protection of health or morals, or for the protection of the rights and freedoms of others.

ARTICLE 9
FREEDOM OF THOUGHT, CONSCIENCE AND RELIGION

1. Everyone has the right to freedom of thought, conscience and religion; this right includes freedom to change his religion or belief, and freedom, either alone or in community with others and in public or private, to manifest his religion or belief, in worship, teaching, practice and observance.
2. Freedom to manifest one's religion or beliefs shall be subject only to such limitations as are prescribed by law and are necessary in a democratic society in the interests of public safety, for the protection of public order, health or morals, or for the protection of the rights and freedoms of others.

ARTICLE 10
FREEDOM OF EXPRESSION

1. Everyone has the right to freedom of expression. This right shall include freedom to hold opinions and to receive and impart information and ideas without interference by public authority and regardless of frontiers. This Article shall not prevent states from requiring the licensing of broadcasting, television or cinema enterprises.
2. The exercise of these freedoms, since it carries with it duties and responsibilities, may be subject to such formalities, conditions, restrictions or penalties as are prescribed by law and are necessary in a democratic society, in the interests of national security, territorial integrity or public safety, for the prevention of disorder or crime, for the protection of health or morals, for the protection of the reputation or rights of others, for preventing the disclosure of information received in confidence, or for maintaining the authority and impartiality of the judiciary.

ARTICLE 11
FREEDOM OF ASSEMBLY AND ASSOCIATION

1. Everyone has the right to freedom of peaceful assembly and to freedom of association with others, including the right to form and to join trade unions for the protection of his interests.

2. No restrictions shall be placed on the exercise of these rights other than such as are prescribed by law and are necessary in a democratic society in the interests of national security or public safety, for the prevention of disorder or crime, for the protection of health or morals or for the protection of the rights and freedoms of others. This Article shall not prevent the imposition of lawful restrictions on the exercise of these rights by members of the armed forces, of the police or of the administration of the state.

ARTICLE 12
RIGHT TO MARRY
Men and women of marriageable age have the right to marry and to found a family, according to the national laws governing the exercise of this right.

ARTICLE 14
PROHIBITION OF DISCRIMINATION
The enjoyment of the rights and freedoms set forth in this Convention shall be secured without discrimination on any ground such as sex, race, colour, language, religion, political or other opinion, national or social origin, association with a national minority, property, birth or other status.

ARTICLE 16
RESTRICTIONS ON POLITICAL ACTIVITY OF ALIENS
Nothing in Articles 10, 11 and 14 shall be regarded as preventing the High Contracting Parties from imposing restrictions on the political activity of aliens.

ARTICLE 17
PROHIBITION OF ABUSE OF RIGHTS
Nothing in this Convention may be interpreted as implying for any state, group or person any right to engage in any activity or perform any act aimed at the destruction of any of the rights and freedoms set forth herein or at their limitation to a greater extent than is provided for in the Convention.

ARTICLE 18
LIMITATION ON USE OF RESTRICTIONS ON RIGHTS
The restrictions permitted under this Convention to the said rights and freedoms shall not be applied for any purpose other than those for which they have been prescribed.

Part II The first protocol

ARTICLE 1
PROTECTION OF PROPERTY
Every natural or legal person is entitled to the peaceful enjoyment of his possessions. No one shall be deprived of his possessions except in the public

interest and subject to the conditions provided for by law and by the general principles of international law. The preceding provisions shall not, however, in any way impair the right of a state to enforce such laws as it deems necessary to control the use of property in accordance with the general interest or to secure the payment of taxes or other contributions or penalties.

ARTICLE 2
RIGHT TO EDUCATION

No person shall be denied the right to education. In the exercise of any functions which it assumes in relation to education and to teaching, the state shall respect the right of parents to ensure such education and teaching in conformity with their own religious and philosophical convictions.

ARTICLE 3
RIGHT TO FREE ELECTIONS (OMITTED)

Part III The sixth protocol

[Containing Article 1 (abolition of the death penalty) and Article 2 (death penalty in time of war) (OMITTED)]

Index of cases referenced in footnotes

Case reference	Footnote
Buckley v UK (1994) 18 EHRR CD 123	136, 196, 198, 200
Burton v UK (1996) 22 EHRR CD 135	136
C v UK (1987) 54 DR 162	66
Campbell and Cosans v UK 4 EHRR 293	78
Campbell and Fell v UK (1984) 7 EHRR 165	112, 114
Castells v Spain [1992] 14 EHRR 445	95
Cavalier v Pope [1906] AC 428	231
Clingham, see R v Marylebone Magistrates Court ex parte Clingham	
Cocks v Thanet District Council [1983] 2 AC 286, HL	56
Costello-Roberts v UK (1993) 19 EHRR 192	69
Coyne v UK RJD 1997-V 1842	112
D v Council, unreported, case T-264/97, 28 January 1998	249
Da Silva Mouta see Silva Mouta v Portugal	
Darnell v UK (1991) 69 DR 306	66
Donoghue v Poplar Housing and Regeneration Company & The Secretary of State for the Environment, Transport and the Regions [2001] EWCA Civ 595	51, 52, 54, 55, 56, 177, 187, 191, 194
Dudgeon v UK (1981) 4 EHRR 149	94, 96, 126
Eckle v FRG (1982) 5 EHRR 1	77,79
Feeldbrugge v The Netherlands (1986) 8 EHRR 425	105
Findlay v UK (1997) 24 EHRR 227	112
Fitzpatrick v Sterling Housing Association [1999] 3 WLR 1113	123, 242, 249
Gallacher v Stirling Council, unreported, Court of Session, 2 May 2000	181
Gaskin case 10454/83	252
Geoffrey, Ptr 16 March 2000	173
Gillow v UK (1986) 11 EHRR 335	102, 131, 152
Grant v South West Trains [1998] All ER (EC) 193, ECJ	249
Guerra v Italy (1998) 26 EHRR 357	227
Gul v Switzerland (1996) 22 EHRR 93	137

Case reference	Footnote
H v Belgium (1987) 10 EHRR 339	100
Halford v UK (1997) 24 EHRR 523	66
Harrogate BC v Simpson (1984) 17 HLR 205	138, 244, 246, 249
Hoffman v Austria (1993) 17 EHRR 293	151
Howard v UK (1987) 52 DR 198	132, 133, 141, 164, 169
Hussain v Lancaster City Council [2000] 1 QB 1	210, 214
Iatridis v Greece, unreported, 25 March 1999, ECHR	159
Immobilarie Saffri v Italy (2000) 30 EHRR 756	167
James v UK (1986) 8 EHRR 123	93, 109, 153, 162, 165, 168, 171
Johns, see R (on the application of Johns & McLellan) v Bracknell Forest District Council	
Johnston v Ireland (1986) 9 EHRR 203	96, 120
Kaur v Lord Advocate 1981 SLT 322	12
Larkos v Cyprus (1999) 7 BHRC 244	149, 188
Lindsay and Lindsay v UK (1986) 49 DR 181	146
Liverpool City Council v Irwin [1977] AC 239	229
Loizidou v Turkey (1995) 20 EHRR 99	131
Lambeth LBC v Howard [2001] EWCA Civ 468	225
Lopez-Ostra v Spain (1995) 20 EHRR 277	127, 134, 226
McCann, see R (on the application of McCann) v Manchester Crown Court	
Malone, case 8691/79	252
Marckx v Belgium (1979) 2 EHRR	120
Mazari v Italy 1999 28 EHRR CD 175	200
McPhee v North Lanarkshire Council 1998 SLT 1317	195
Mellacher v Austria (1989) 12 EHRR 391	158, 159, 166, 168, 240
Mowan v Wandsworth & Another (2001) 33 HLR 56	69, 73, 211, 212, 214, 216

Case reference	Footnote
Neimietz v Germany (1992) 16 EHRR 97	126
Nelson v UK (1986) 49 DR 181	147
Oakley v Birmingham City Council (2001) 33 HLR 30	239
O'Reilly v Mackman [1983] 2 AC 237, HL	56
O'Rourke v Camden LBC [1998] AC 188, HL	56
Olsson v Sweden (no. 2) (1992) 17 EHRR 134	104
Peabody Housing Association v Greene (1978) 38 P&CR. 644	56
Powell and Rayner v UK (1990) 12 EHRR 355	110, 128, 214
Quick v Taff Ely BC [1986] QB 809	230
R (on the application of Alconbury Developments and others) v Secretary of State for the Environment, Transport and the Regions, unreported, 13 December 2000 case reference CO/3742/2000	116, 199, 202
R (on the application of Johns & McLellan) v Bracknell Forest District Council, [2001] 33 HLR 45	44, 116, 172, 186, 188, 199, 201, 202
R (on the application of McCann) v Manchester Crown Court [2001] EWCA Civ 281	44, 172, 192, 221, 222, 224
R v Home Secretary, ex parte Brind [1991] 1 AC 696 at 747	12
R v Khan [1996] 1 WLR 162	12
R v Marylebone Magistrates Court ex parte Clingham [2001] EWCA ADMIN 1	192, 223
R v Panel on Take-overs and Mergers, ex parte Datafin [1987] QB 815, CA	56
R v West Dorset Housing Association, ex parte Gerrard (1994) 27 HLR 150	56
Rayner v UK (1986) 47 DR 5	128
Rees v UK 9 EHRR 56	72
Robb v HMA 18 March 2000	173
S v UK (1986) 47 DR 274	138, 150, 237, 244, 246
Salesi v Italy (1993) Series A, No. 257-E	105
Schuler-Zgraggen v Switzerland (1993) 16 EHRR 405	105

Case reference	Footnote
Scollo v Italy (1995) 22 EHRR 514	167
Silva Mouta v Portugal ECHR, 21 December 1999	122, 249
Silver v UK (1983) 5 EHRR 347	89, 142
Smith v Marrable (1843) 11 M&W 5	231
Southwark LBC v Mills (2000) 32 HLR 148	231
Spadea and Scalabrino v Italy (1995) 21 EHRR 482	154, 158, 167, 168
Sporrong and Lönnroth v Sweden (1982) 5 EHRR 35	93, 103
Starrs and Chalmers v Ruxton 2000 JC 208	112, 173
Stefan v UK (1997) 25 EHRR CD 130	199
Stewart v Inverness District Council 1992 SLT 690	195
Sunday Times v UK (1979) 2 EHRR 245	142
Sutherland v UK [1996] EHLRR 554	247
Tre Traktörer Aktiebolag v Sweden (1989) 13 EHRR 309	101
Van Mehlen v Netherlands 23 April 1997, RJD, 1997-111, No. 56	87
Velosa Barretto v Portugal (1995)	158
West v Secretary of State for Scotland 1992 SC 385	65
Whiteside v UK (1994) 76 – A DR 80	213
Wiggins v UK (1978) 13 DR 40	132
X v Federal Republic of Germany (1956) 1 YB 202	135, 197
X v Iceland (1976) 5 DR 86	129
X v UK (1998) 25 EHRR CD 88	199
X, Y and Z v UK (1997) 24 EHRR 143	97, 124

Some key housing cases decided under the Human Rights Act 1998

(For full case reference see table in Appendix 2)

Case	Issues considered	Outcome
Alconbury	Requirement to refer planning decisions to Secretary of State. Town and Country Planning Act 1990, s.77	• Judicial review is not sufficient to remedy unfair hearing where the person whose decision is being reviewed is also the principle policy maker. In the case of planning appeals both the policy and the appeal is decided by the Secretary of State. Legislation incompatible with Convention. • Although the legislation is incompatible the Secretary of State not acting unlawfully (Human Rights Act 1998 s.6(2)).
Bates	Possession proceedings for anti-social behaviour. Extent to which the defendant must be allowed to prepare their defence for a trial to be fair.	• Article 6 will be breached if tenant is not given a proper opportunity to seek advice about their defence especially in cases where skilled representation likely to make a real difference to the outcome. • Legal representation likely to make a real difference to outcome of trial where credibility of witnesses is likely to be a significant factor (e.g. anti-social behaviour).
Clingham	Anti-social behaviour orders. Whether use of civil procedures for obtaining order are fair. Crime and Disorder Act 1998, s1.	• Civil proceedings for obtaining ASBO are not unfair. There is no presumption in the Convention of a right to cross-examine witnesses or against the use of hearsay evidence in civil trials. • Civil proceedings are fair because the court is to act in a way which is compatible with the Convention.
Donoghue	Whether RSLs are public authorities. What activities are public functions. Human Rights Act 1998, s6.	• Ordinary core activities of RSLs will not normally be considered public functions despite the fact that the RSL may have been formed by LSVT from the parent authority. • RSLs will only be public bodies in relation to a limited range of activities which have a particular "public stamp or character".

Case	Issues considered	Outcome
Donoghue – contd.		• In determining whether a particular activity is a public function regard should be had as to the extent to which the activity is "enmeshed in the activities of a public body". • RSLs assisting a local authority with homelessness duty pending its enquiries (including recovering possession following adverse decision) likely to be carrying out a public function.
Johns	Introductory Tenancies. Whether legislation and use of introductory tenancies is compatible with the Convention. Housing Act 1996, Part V, ss 124-130	• Internal review process does not meet the standard of fairness and impartiality required but judicial sufficient to remedy the defect because the decision could be quashed if the reviewer acted on no evidence or reached an unreasonable conclusion. • Eviction procedure for introductory tenancies does interfere with the right to respect for the home (Article 8) but the legislation is within the margin of appreciation because it is necessary and proportionate. • Although the Introductory tenancy legislation conforms with the Convention because it does not compel the authority to act disproportionately the use of the procedure may be disproportionate in a particular case depending on the facts (e.g. if they acted on no evidence or used them oppressively). • Introductory tenancies apply to all new tenants so not discriminatory.
McCann	Anti-social behaviour Orders. Whether legislation compatible with Convention. Is procedure civil or criminal? Crime and Disorder Act 1998, s1.	• Procedures for obtaining anti-social behaviour orders (ASBOs) are civil and not criminal so the subject is not entitled to the minimum rights afforded by Article 6(2) and 6(3). • ASBO legislation does not itself breach the Convention. • Use of ASBO powers in a particular case may infringe the Convention so the principle of proportionality must be observed.
Mowan	Nuisance created by one local authority tenant against another. Does Human Rights Act create a new duty for the local authority to act?	• Human Rights Act does not create a new common law duty for the local authority to act, since aggrieved tenant has remedy in private nuisance. Rule that landlord is not responsible for own tenants nuisance unless they have authorised it, confirmed.

Human Rights for Housing Officers: A Guide to Proofing Day-to-day Practice

(CIH/JRF forthcoming, spring 2002).

Kate Tongue, Trevor Grundy and Tony Stark

This forthcoming publication is designed to complement *A Guide to the Human Rights Act 1998 for Housing Professionals*. Its purpose is to describe a methodology that will enable practitioners to scrutinise day-to-day aspects of housing policy and practice with respect to the Human Rights Act. In addition to expert legal advice the Guide describes a practical audit process which is designed to help practitioners understand, assess and reduce the risk of a human rights challenge.

The Guide draws on the practical experience and ideas arising from extensive training sessions conducted with housing departments and RSLs over a six month period following the introduction of the Act. The Guide is designed to be used as a training aid for housing organisations and their staff, as well as councillors, RSL board members and their residents.

> **Kate Tonge** is an independent welfare law consultant specialising solely in housing and social security. She provides technical advice and assistance to a number of local authority housing departments, housing benefit departments and registered social landlords.
>
> She is co-author and co-editor of Butterworth's *Welfare Law* series and editor of Tolley's *Social Security State Benefits Handbook*. She is a Law Society approved provider of training for housing and social security law to the legal profession. She qualified in 1984.
>
> **Trevor Grundy** is a senior member of the Bolton MBC legal team that was recently given a maximum "3 Star" rating by the Best Value Inspectorate. He is a Fellow of the Institute of Legal Executives with over 30 years experience of public sector law. He is an active member of a Law Society Local Government Group and is the author of Bolton's award winning tenancy agreement. He is also a member of Clarity – an organisation to promote plain language in the law.
>
> **Tony Stark**, is a solicitor in private practice and a part time Deputy District Judge.

Available: Spring 2002 from CIH publications, Coventry. Tel: 024 7685 1764/1752.

CHARTERED INSTITUTE OF HOUSING

A 20% discount will apply when you send this coupon with your order for *Human Rights for Housing Officers*.
Discount limited to one book only.
Valid until 30 September 2002.